Beyond The
Pretty
Dress

BEYOND THE PRETTY DRESS
E. Claudette Freeman, Editor

ISBN: 978-1-7328311-3-1 (Paperback)
ISBN: 978-1-7328311-4-8 (Digital)
Library of Congress Control Number: 2018959199

All scriptures listed are King James Version or New International Version.

Cover Design by Haley James

Editor's Photo - Ashley Jackson, BRF Productions

Book interior design by Jenette Antonio Sityar

Freeman Thomas Books
Pecan Tree Publishing
Hollywood, FL 33020

FREEMAN THOMAS BOOKS,
A PECAN TREE PUBLISHING IMPRINT

PECAN TREE PUBLISHING

www.pecantreebooks.com
info@pecantreebooks.com

Table of Contents

Beyond The
Pretty
Dress

Scriptural Encouragement

Strength and honour are her clothing;
and she shall rejoice in time to come.

PROVERBS 31:25

Let nothing be done through strife or vain glory;
but in lowliness of mind let each esteem other better than
themselves. Look not every man on his own things,
but every man also on the things of others. Let this mind be in
you, which was also in Christ Jesus.

PHILIPPIANS 2:3-5

Foreword

ANIKA WILSON BROWN

BE CAREFUL IN YOUR PRETTY DRESS

One of the best compliments that a girl can receive is "wow, that is a beautiful dress!" I remember being flattered by those words as a child. Each time I heard it, I'd blush and giggle as I proudly took a glance at the beautiful dress that mommy had made or purchased for that day. Pretty dresses always made me feel good because of the approval that I would get from others.

The dress is a symbol of femininity, grace and style in American culture. It can be a tool for unique expression of identity and style. But for many women, the dress may also represent the oppression of gender roles, restriction of religious expectations and the limitations on career or other goals in life. For some, the dress can also represent traumatic violations of boundaries and unrestricted access to secret places.

As I reviewed the chronicles of the various women who are captured in this book, I began to question what was behind my own pretty dress. As a pastor and mental health counselor, I know that there is power in self-reflection. My self-reflection led me to ask how something so pretty could also be the source of so much pain?

I began to recall my own experiences. One stood out vividly...

One hot Sunday around 1982, I remember anxiously waiting for church to end. My mom used to put the prettiest dresses on me. As the pastors' eldest daughter, I learned early that image was everything! It was important to look "put together" on Sunday mornings. I enjoyed looking pretty, but there was a special freedom that I looked forward to each week; and it had nothing to do with my pretty dress!

I sat on the wooden pews with my thumb in my mouth; I could hardly wait for the last amen. Immediately, I'd get permission and run straight to the playground, which was behind our church. "Be careful in your pretty dress," onlookers would shout as I ran past them, toward the monkey bars. Their words usually caused me to slow the pace of my jovial jog to a thoughtful trot.

I had two best friends at my church and both of them happened to be boys. I watched them with envy, once we reached the edge of the playground. They always seemed to get to the playground first. Not because they were faster, but because I had on a pretty dress. I didn't mind them beating me to the playground, but my excitement would be followed by restraint once we reached the sliding board. My friends never stopped, they always kept going once we got there. They seemed to have no burdens at all as they laughed, climbed, and played with reckless abandon.

Watching from the side, I'd giggle, clasping the hem of my pretty dress. The prettiness of my dress almost felt like a prison.

My play was clouded with cautiousness. I wanted to run and jump so badly. I wanted to run wild. I wanted to play with them... but mostly, I wanted to play LIKE them! They seemed to have no cares in the world. Nobody told them not to climb too high. Or not to spread their legs too wide. They didn't receive the warnings, not to run too fast or they would scuff their knees. Nobody judged their freedom.

On this particular Sunday, I decided that the pretty dress wouldn't stop me. I looked back to see who was watching as I slowly began to climb the ladder that led to the top of the monkey bars.!

I didn't care who saw me!

I didn't care what anyone said!

I didn't care if my purple panties were visible as I swung my legs trying to make it to the next bar.

My legs dangled, and my hands were burning hot from the sting of gripping the monkey bars so tightly, but I never felt so free!! I laughed, I ran and jumped. It was one of my sweetest memories.

10

... until one of the mean ladies at church rolled her eyes at me and reprimanded me.

Her words were cold, "Girls don't play like that, you are going to ruin your pretty dress!"

What happens when you no longer feel at home in the pretty dress that you wear?

What happens when the prettiness becomes a prison that limits the true expression of who you are?

What happens when, instead of compliments, you receive criticism?

As a pastor and mental health counselor, I find myself working with women of various ages and life circumstances, most of them have one thing in common. Women always seem to be searching for their identity in a world that wants to define them and restrict them to who they SHOULD be. Identity, reputation and expectations is often a component of my spiritual and therapeutic work with women. Consequently, I have found that maintaining the image of a pretty dress can be a source of trauma and internal conflict for many women. Sometimes, women choose to align with what is expected of them, no matter how much stress and anguish it causes them. On occasion, it's too risky to be revolutionary and women may decide that it's easier to do what's expected.

Let's face it, women are often celebrated for their appearances rather than their audaciousness. Consequently it takes an act of courage for a woman to reveal who she is behind the façade, behind the pretty dress! Who are you Behind the Pretty Dress? This book will liberate you to explore that very question.

Beyond the Pretty Dress highlights the stories of bold warrior women who resist stereotypical expectations through acts of reckless abandon. In many cases, this meant radical shifts in their religious and spiritual identities women of God. You will hear the stories of pastors, first ladies and ministry leaders who dared to live and serve Beyond the Pretty Dress. These radical acts often served as a catalyst for greater intimacy with God. These bold women stepped outside of the limitation of tradition and religious rules to create a deeper intimacy with Christ that was based on what they had experienced and not just what someone expected of them.

Pecan Publishing is known for curating literary works for progressive thinkers who are not afraid to grow! This work is no different! It challenges us to look beyond images and perceptions and step into the realm of possibility. Beyond the Pretty Dress articulates the narratives of women who are often overlooked because they don't fit in, giving value to the unique expression that every woman is!!

As you read, your life will be transformed as you see life through the lenses of these powerful women. Missionary Janice Lewis will challenge you to step out of the comfort zone of what is familiar to truly tap into your soul's purpose. Cyteria Freeman will introduce you to the power of resilience against all odds, inspiring you to be aware of the power to overcome any obstacle that you face in life. Chosen Thummims' story will expand your thinking beyond the religions assumptions that divide us as she shares her journey of merging Christian and Muslim faiths. Her story will teach you the universality of God and the power of intercessory prayer to overcome all disharmony. Every story will expand and challenge you.

I have been both enlightened and encouraged by these stories and I have no doubt that you will also.

As you read, I pray that you will do as I did on that playground, over 30 years ago. Play... Live.... Serve... and do so with reckless abandonment of the limitations and restrictions that others have placed upon you.

Pastor Anika Wilson-Brown, MSW, LGSW
www.anikawilsonbrown.com
Washington, DC

A Poetic Push

I've Stepped Over And Beyond The Pretty Dress

by E. Chantaye Watson

You see me coming
I look just like you
But, the streets my pulpit
While it don't look like
what a good Christian do...

I know I got that smile
And I walk like I'm blessed
Ah, but if you only knew
the struggle
beyond the pretty dress...

I roll up in transparency
I tell my story
It's enough to give you hope but God gets all the glory

God knew we would meet
So, He fashioned my test
And gave me
the strength and the courage
beyond the pretty dress

It's in His grace I walk Free ain't always free Jesus paid the cost
for this liberty...

Don't let the smile fool ya
I've gone through some mess
I've step over things that killed others beyond this pretty dress

Who you are inspires me
The possibility of my God sure
I won't judge or look down on you
I thank God for how you've endured
The things that you've been going through today God will put it to rest
I'm a living witness of restoration
beyond the pretty dress.

Lord, Don't Let Me Die Like This

CYTERIA FREEMAN

"**P**umpkin! Pumpkin! Stop it now! Come on over here! Enough is enough now. Act right and come here."

The monster was raging again. I was on another seething trip driven by my high. Fighting was not an unusual thing for me. I was a fighter. All you had to do was look at me wrong, or for that matter all I had to do was think you looked at me wrong and I was ready to fight. The fighting would intensify if you spoke to me in a manner that I considered harsh. Hello, honestly, could have sounded harsh to me depending on the level of my feel good at that moment.

"Pumpkin get in the car! Get in the car now!"

The voice of my brother-in-law's nephew still bangs in my ears so clearly. He would pick me up off the streets so many times for fighting. His voice would be so loud and stern from his patrol car loud speaker.

"Pumpkin, Pumpkin you gonna get arrested for disorderly conduct. Come here; come get in the car right now!"

I would stumble to the car still talking trash, still ready to fight and yet respecting his authority and the fact that he would not take me to jail. Instead he would take me to family – my sister or my mom. I am sure he wished they would find a way to keep me out of the streets before another police officer grew tired of my foolishness. I mean everybody knew Pumpkin and everybody knew I would fight – with or without reason. I remember several times when a former lover would come looking for me after I would be gone from home and my children for days on end. His discovery of me would always lead to arguments; arguments would always lead to fist fights. I imagine we would have been one of the featured fights passed around on social media if that type of thing was popular then.

> ## MATTHEW 8:16
>
> "When the even was come, they brought unto him many that were possessed with devils: and he cast out the spirits with his word and healed all that were sick:"

Then, was the late 70's/early 80's. I was living the high life. My high life did not entail big fancy cars, extravagant housing full of the latest from the interior design industry. My high life was just that – days of getting high, higher and higher still. My high life was an excruciating descent into hell at the invitation of the demon that kept seducing everything I was convinced I needed.

MATTHEW 8:16

"When the even was come, they brought unto him many that were possessed with devils: and he cast out the spirits with his word and healed all that were sick:" In the tenderness of my 15th year of life, I gave birth to my first child and stepped into the spiraling effects of so much emotional upheaval. Growing up in the South Side projects of Daytona Beach, Florida, I had come familiar with rejection. My Daytona was not the one marketed on tourism brochures attracting the large motorcycle gangs that would gather. It was not the beach beautiful city where throngs of high school and college students would flock looking for a party and sensual romance

with no questions asked. It was the projects, where the money was low, the crime was high and whatever you needed to drown your sorrows was readily available.

My first baby daddy loved me enough to get my most precious gift, and then he dumped me and disrespected me like I was nothing more than a two-dollar one night stand he had paid for. The rejection hit me hard; so hard in fact that I dropped out of Spruce Creek High School; the place where I should have learned so much more about history and algebra. Instead I experienced the painful lessons of a broken heart and took a class in the wrong things to heal the pain. I just could not take the nasty remarks and the even more vicious looks. A friend introduced me to this club, where no one cared what kind of baggage you came in with me, I was a young thing with a nice smile and the men gave me all kinds of wonderful attention. I loved that attention. The club became my classroom and I became one of its best students.

I began to go through all kind of experiences and dealt with all kinds of people. No one was a stranger to me. I considered everybody a friend even those that chose to live a homosexual life style. I always had love and compassion for people; so much so that on occasion I would allow different females to live with me. One of those acts of compassion introduced me to yet another heart break experience, when I discovered she felt so comfortable in my home that she became comfortable in my relationship as well. My heart shattered into a thousand pieces when I found out that she was sleeping with my man. After that there was no reason to continue in either relationship. I began to go on this rollercoaster ride in and out of relationships with no sense of direction I began having baby after baby from different men. This was the beginning of a degree I earned from being in the streets. In the streets, you learn things that no text book can teach you. The name of the game is survival and only the strong survive.

It was around the time that the 70's sashayed off the scene and allowed the 80's to take their place, that the projects and the streets of Daytona Beach were abuzz with this new thing. The projects where I lived surely resemble those in other urban neighborhoods across America. The neighborhood was full of rows of housing units that were almost carbon copies of each other. The neighborhood burst at the seams with poor and lower income middle in the actual project units; and middle-class families in the small but nicer houses that were built on the perimeter of the projects.

The projects were already the place to help your feel-good feel even better, but I do not believe even South Street Projects was ready for what this new little rock formed drug was about to bring. This new thing promised an escape from everything that life was handing you that you did not want to deal with. The formal invitation to the central Florida community came at the hands of a drug boy out of Miami. He said it was going to make money and it was going to make everyone who kissed it feel lovely.

I could have taken him at his word but that was not good enough. He made this hot commodity sound better than any product promoted by a well-paid advertising agent. I liked his advertisement and bought into what he was selling - literally. As the drug started flowing from corner to corner, my sister and I were in the thick of it. She was younger than me and had already dibbled and dabbled in different narcotics. It was no surprise to me (or her) that she too was fascinated with this new high they called crack cocaine. We started using and selling this drug for Miami. Then I started using it for the thrill of it. I loved the way crack cocaine made me feel. It would send tingles through me. It was more enticing than the touch of any lover and it had no ill words to speak to me or of me. It felt sweet and then it allowed me to become numb. Crack cocaine became the high of choice in my diet of street pharmaceuticals. Do not take the fact that I refer to it as a diet lightly. For a diet is merely the combination of a daily intake of substance - usually food. For me, the 80's and early 90's found me on a diet of drugs that maintained my life.

On my journey to my master, I would get up, get dressed and leave the house at 1 or 2 in the morning to walk to down to the bottom. Funny, certainly most of us have had a parent or older family member say nothing good happens in the dark; and you can't find anything but trouble hanging out in the middle of night. It is funny, in an ironic kind of way, because I would get dressed for the dark like I was getting dressed to get to my morning job. I would walk through the darkest section of the Southside projects all by myself. Had the call to get high not been so strong my common sense would have prevailed in its advance warnings. Those warnings would remind me about the number of women, some drug users and some not, who had disappeared in Daytona during the era that I would take my past midnight strolls.

Some of these girls were found in the woods right off the path where I was walking; others were found raped (sometimes with foreign objects like soda bottles) and beaten to death near the pier. A strange chill moved across my body as I remember one especially frightening warning. I was walking in middle of the road, the woods and the path around me. I was alone on this road because I had not gone that far from the projects and I had checked my surroundings. Suddenly, I heard something say, "You need to turn around." I looked all around me again, there was no one. But the voice persisted, because I was still trying to get there, to my high. Something in the persistence grabbed me and the second time it spoke to me; I heard this voice say, "It is too late, go back home." As soon as the voice grew quiet I could not go any further, not because I did not want to but because physically I could not. It was like something was in the middle of the street, standing right in front of me and would not let me go pass that spot. So, I finally turned around. The next day they found a girl dead on the pier. Even on the path to death, there was a power pulling me to life and am thankful that I listened to its voice; had I not, you would not have this living testament to the fact that overcoming is an option and it is the choice to live.

***

With three kids at home, the taste of crack cocaine in my system, a new man in my life – I was with baby number four. That was a wild relationship. We were both drug users and drank alcohol every day. We would fight all the time and he would cheat as much as we would fight. Before I knew it, we were being evicted. I was not paying bills because whatever money I did have, or I could get hold to had to go to crack. I could not explain it to anyone or even to myself, but I knew that if I didn't give crack my money, he would not give me my high, my love, my peace and I would not be able to rest in the place of not feeling anything. I didn't care that I was not going to have a place to live. My kids were safe with my mom and he could be a daddy to his child. I had to get high.

I was so out of control and so high one day before the eviction was final. The kids were at home with me. He and I got into a thing and I lost my mind.

The details of it all are still blurry in my conscious mind; but I know that the situation got so bad that he called the police. I do not know if the call was to protect him, protect the kids or protect me – yet there they were. Their presence meant nothing to me. I was so high; and I was fighting. I was fighting him; and I was fighting the police. They sprayed mace on me and still they couldn't get me in the car. Then I was a small girl, about five feet, seven inches tall and only about 140 pounds. Yet, at that size, not even their strength or the sting of the mace on my skin could control me. Crack had me convinced at that moment that he had my back and we were fighting all of them together. I had to be stopped because I was going to jail, there was no deterring it this time. They pulled out their blackjacks, but before they hit me – they, like I, heard my kids yelling.

"Mommy please, stop. Mommy, stop. Do not hit my mommy please. Mommy please just get in the car, mommy please."

A moment of sanity and clarity hit me; and I saw the pain and anguish pouring out in tears; I released the fight. Still, I descended deeper into hell. Each step I took, crack held me firmly around my waist escorting wonderfully into his destruction. He knew how to keep a lady's attention and to destroy her family in the process.

I was the epitome of the black sheep. I was one that had the most kids and started at such an early age. I was the one that was very blatant and wild with my drug use. I think most of my family is still ashamed of me. So now those of us who were considered the outcasts stick together. The ones that felt like they were better, or in an upper class, do not really associate with us. There were times we would go weeks or months without talking to each other. That was not the prayer my mother placed before a God who had already assured her restoration is possible.

When the invitation to finally be free came to me after the birth of my fifth child, I found a passage of scripture that I would read and read and read. I felt like I had to absorb it so that it oozed like sweat from my pores. That passage is Romans 8, part of it reads like this.

> "There is therefore now no condemnation to them which are in Christ Jesus, who walk not after the flesh, but after the Spirit.

For the law of the Spirit of life in Christ Jesus hath made me free from the law of sin and death. For what the law could not do, in that it was weak through the flesh, God sending his own Son in the likeness of sinful flesh, and for sin, condemned sin in the flesh: That the righteousness of the law might be fulfilled in us, who walk not after the flesh, but after the Spirit. For they that are after the flesh do mind the things of the flesh; but they that are after the Spirit the things of the Spirit. For to be carnally minded is death; but to be spiritually minded is life and peace. Because the carnal mind is enmity against God: for it is not subject to the law of God, neither indeed can be. So, then they that are in the flesh cannot please God. But ye are not in the flesh, but in the Spirit, if so be that the Spirit of God dwells in you. Now if any man have not the Spirit of Christ, he is none of his. And if Christ be in you, the body is dead because of sin; but the Spirit is life because of righteousness. But if the Spirit of him that raised up Jesus from the dead dwell in you, he that raised up Christ from the dead shall also quicken your mortal bodies by his Spirit that dwelleth in you."

***

Even in our descent into the gates of hell, God will reach out to you and spare your life. For while the fire burns us, it is nothing more than light tickles to Him. It has no power and no sting to the Most High God. Through my dance with the devil, God's hand was forever upon me. So many people I grew up with got hooked on the same crack introduced to me. Some became prostitutes on the corners, the bodies hanging free for the advantage of anyone and sometimes all that anyone needed was a five-dollar bill. Here I was set up in every possible situation where any of a long list of sexually transmitted diseases could have and should have invaded my body.

When I would leave the streets, I would go back to an empty apartment. I would stumble into the bathroom in the apartment and glance at the image of a creature in the mirror. I would realize that creature was me. I would cry behind closed doors and say, "Lord do not let no one see me like this, do not let me die looking like this. Do not ever let my kids see me like this."

I would get by myself and look in the mirror and I would say, "Lord, these drugs have taken control of my body and they are living in me." I would stay away on purpose, believing my absence was better for them. When I came to know God's full deliverance; I thought about the Word of God that warns us a one demon goes and gets seven others in his inhabitation. The longer I committed adultery with the demonic crack, the more my countenance became the likeness of the imp that controlled me for the moment.

One morning I was up getting high, a very normal routine for me; it was an especially bright morning and as much as I can remember about it, it was equally still. I sat in the room getting high and suddenly the brightness of that room hid beneath darkness. The room got dark. This was not the dim mood that moves in temporarily when the clouds move in front of the sun; this was utter darkness. It was as though night had come at a moment's notice. I looked around the dark room, trying to figure out if I was tripping. Had I gotten a bad cut of the rock or was it laced with some hallucinogenic? In the darkness, all I could see was snakes; snakes on the walls, on the curtains and on the door. There were snakes on everything in the room where I sat. Some were alive and others dead, but they were all jabbing at me. They were all coming after me. There was a light around me, but I was terrified, and I heard something say if you have enough faith to open that door you will not have to worry about drugs anymore. Somehow, I opened the door and when I came to my senses I was on the other side of the projects, but facing my apartment there was no one around. I ran back to my apartment. And I told God if he took the drugs out of my mouth that I would do whatever he wanted me to.

I learned something about God and about His deliverance. You must participate in that deliverance. The first time I went into treatment I missed that valuable lesson. You see the first time I went into treatment I was depending too much on me and not enough on God. I figured I had it all together. I had done what they asked me to and I had been clean for eight months. That time in treatment had dug up some stuff in me. I had to face the hard reality of being the kind of woman that would feed her unborn child crack cocaine. A year and half of being clean, I felt my "strength". I wanted to show everyone that I was bigger than the drugs. I wanted to prove that I could still be around the users and the dealers and not smoke crack. I fooled myself. It started with sharing a soda or two with some of the old gang. Sharing a soda led to sharing a beer and one drink here and there; I quickly graduated again to the head of the class and for five more years crack and I tangoed once again.

In 1995, the demon had no choice but to flee. I had made up my mind for God. I had decided that I was going to accept every prayer that my mother had lifted for me and I knew that God was honoring every scream to help me that I had ever yelled out – even though I was high during most of those pleas. At night, headaches and bad dreams would wrestle with me. The dreams would taunt me, "you are an addict, you can't get off drug, you are scum, you are low, come on back and get high." The demon forgot that I am a fighter and I fought back every night until there were no headaches and no bad dreams.

I was probably a different kind of cat for the counselors and psychologists in the treatment centers. The bulk of the counseling indicates that you are a "recovering" or "overcoming" addict. They would say once an addict, always an addict. I had to reject that notion for me. I had to accept that God set me free and so I was free. I am a former addict. I am now redeemed, forgiven and delivered. I actively participate in my deliverance. That means I stay in the word of God, I minister to those I used to get high with in safe boundaries, I profess what I used to be and then glorify God for what I am.

I found what I was looking for in drugs, alcohol and sex at the funeral of some young men we knew growing up. Bishop Derek T. Triplett, Pastor of Hope Fellowship Ministries in Daytona Beach, preached a eulogy that changed and saved my life. From there I become part of the intercessory prayer ministry and became a minister-in-training and finally an ordained minister. God changed my life so powerfully that I received my minister's license in August of 2001. My sister Patricia and I went on to start a radio ministry, and a ministry where we walk the streets looking for those who are living the testimony we once did. We share their pain. We hear their stores. We pray without judgment, because we were them. I rebuke the devil from them, like I rebuked him from me. My mission is to save as many women and men from that path of demonic narcotic destruction. I would rather they be drugged with the love of Christ than anything else.

I remember a tragedy involving drugs rang out on the evening news in Daytona. A young man beat his father to death because he had refused to give him money to buy drugs. In a drug-induced rage, he beat and stabbed his own father to death. If I could have talked to him, I would tell him to try Christ. The demon he is fighting had escalated his use of him. Only a demonic spirit could cause a son to take his father's life like that.

Drugs are a demon. They are a demon that feed off so many things. There is misguided love, loss of love, rejection, self-esteem, and rape/incest or molestation. Emotional traumas like feeling ignored or misunderstood, unheard can lead to drug use. So now I listen to my grandchildren – and those around me in every circle - differently. I try to listen to hear if there is any pain or lack in what they are saying, and I talk to them up front about what I hear or what I feel they are expressing.

I do not and will not judge anyone's path away from drugs. I will instead pull them out as much as I can. I will offer them the same deliverer that went into the gates of hell for me. I will tell them that I know that I am done with it and they can be too. I am delivered.

When I began my journey into the fullness of Christ, there were ministers, pastors and deacons that tried to minister to me. That ministry however was of little to no effect, because you see while they spoke you need to leave drugs alone, they were yet getting high. My testimony had to be sincere and complete. I could not judge them; but I could not allow them to offer me a false deliverance either.

You have to participate in your deliverance. You may not need deliverance from drugs like I did. You may struggle with pornography or another sexual sin. Perhaps you struggle with being unable to handle your finances – whatever your demon is you can be delivered from it and you must participate in that deliverance. That means face your giants, separate from the unclean things whether they are: friends, family, places or associations. Be strong in Christ and allow Him to be strong in you. I am blessed to have gone from a mess to a miracle to a messenger and this is my message – He who the Son sets free is free indeed, accept His freedom.

CYTERIA'S PRAYER

Heavenly Father, the Most High God, the God of deliverance. I come to you in great faith and in the name of your son Jesus the Christ, asking if you would grant deliverance to everyone who prays this prayer.

I stand upon your Word because your Word is a lamp unto my feet and a light unto my path. Psalms 119: 105 in your Word declares, where the Spirit of the Lord is there is freedom. Second Corinthians 3:17 says and help me not to be entangled again with the yoke of bondage.

And is it is written in your Word in Galatians 5:1, in Jesus name, I bind and take authority over all kinds of addictions – sex, alcohol, crack, cocaine, marijuana and all pharmaceuticals! I gain power, strength and deliverance because whom the Son makes free is free indeed.

In Jesus name, I pray – Amen.

The Road Back to Me

Yvette Freeman Rowland

I was born and raised in Liberty City, more specifically Liberty Square, the Pork & Beans Projects. Liberty City, a predominantly African American community in Miami, Florida – five miles west of the revered South Beach. Liberty Square (colloquially referred to as the Pork & Beans) is a 753-unit Miami-Dade public housing apartment complex in the Liberty City neighborhood of Miami, Florida. It was the first public housing project for blacks in the Southern United States

I lived with my great-grandmother, Mother Gussie Christian. I don't know the events that led to me being in her custody. I never asked, and no one ever shared. Our first location was situated on 62nd Street between 13th and 14th Avenues, in front of the Pool Room that later became Mr. Freddie's Coin Laundry. Granny-great was a devout member of the Historical Mt. Zion Baptist Church in Overtown where the Rev. Edward T. Graham was Senior Pastor. (Overtown, near Downtown Miami, was originally called

Colored Town during the Jim Crow era.) She happily served on several auxiliaries in the church. I really enjoyed being by her side. As a little girl I knew what she was doing was special. She wanted me to know the God she served. She also wanted me to know that Satan and hell were real. The pool room (as she called it) was always full of people, loud music and drama.

Grandma would say with a VERY strong voice, "Vette over there you'll find the devil. And if those fast gals and nasty boys don't get their life right they're going STRAIGHT to hell."

Being a precocious child, my imagination went into overdrive trying to identify which one was the devil. Was he the guy with the crumpled small brown bag taking hearty swigs from a tall green can? Or, maybe the devil was a lady - I pondered. Perhaps the one with the big blonde wig, short skirt, chunky high heels and red lip stick was the devil. Her exaggerated choreographed laugh was quite "interesting." In retrospect, grandma's mission was accomplished. I was sufficiently spooked. I never looked with wonderment in the pool room's direction from THAT day until we moved. As a matter of fact, I have never been attracted to any venues of the type. Proverbs 22:6 does say, "Train up a child in the way he should go: and when he is old, he will not depart from it."

The adolescent years brought lots of changes. Our address changed. We moved around the corner to a bigger unit. Grandma changed into a visibly older and more fragile person. I was constantly haunted with the idea of her dying and what would happen to me. In middle school, classes were changing, it seemed like every other minute. And, everyone's bodies and voices were changing except mine. I still looked and sounded like a baby. I thought it was unfair. I wanted to be a "brickhouse" like the obviously beautiful and shapely woman from The Commodores' song. Everybody in 1977 was singing the R & B song about this woman who was letting it all hang out. It didn't help my self-esteem hearing that song in heavy rotation on Miami's urban-formatted radio station WEDR. Every boom box was blasting it within ear-shot. Whatever this woman had that everyone was singing about, I had nothing to compete with. Those lyrics seemed to taunt me; "how can she lose with the stuff she use? 36-24-36, what a winning hand!" Great, I would think, we all agree that I'm a loser.

I just didn't seem to fit in anywhere. Notwithstanding so many things I wasn't allowed to do or have. Either it wasn't befitting of a child, a child of God, or we just couldn't afford it. Also, I just didn't want to be a burden to my grandmother.

She would make statements like; "you're not going to break my heart like your mother and her mother did, are you?"

My biggest concern with her fear was that , I didn't know what a broken heart was. So, that haunted me too. Thus, began my quest to be this perfect angel that would make my grandma's final days happy. How could I live in a way that would make her feel like she didn't fail? How could I be better than what or who?

When I walked home from school I would experiment with different routes. This gave me the opportunity to survey my community. I loved to walk and observe the people. Liberty City was never lacking as it pertains to "entertainment". It was always SOMETHING jumping-off: a no-holds-barred fist fight on this corner, a very creative compilation of profane exchanges on the other side, the peanut man shouting his daily specials, tires screeching, sirens wailing and the beautiful sounds of the Magic City. According to Miami Historian Dr. Paul George the nickname derived from an article written in the early 1900's by E.V. Blackman. He was encouraged to write a strong, positive story about Miami for Flagler's magazine – "East Coast Homeseeker".

As I matriculated to senior high school, my feeder pattern placed me at Miami Northwestern Senior High. This school has always been steeped in traditions and legacy. It seemed like all the Who's-Who in Miami went to Northwestern and flaunted it. These young men and women had families that were this-and-that. They were beautiful and stylish, boldly arrayed in our school colors, old gold and royal blue. Heck, I barely had lunch money much less the wherewithal to compete in the daily fashion strolls in those hallowed hallways. The feelings of not measuring up to the status quo and the powers that be became ever more prevalent. I did my best to assimilate with my peers, but I always felt like I was swimming upstream. My list of "don't haves" was still growing and everything was looking quite dismal.

My "walks" throughout the city made me inquisitive about life. I said to myself, "there has to be more to life than what I've seen." The more I walked, the more I craved something better. I didn't know what that "something" was or what it meant. I just knew I wanted that feeling to be "somebody" to be fulfilled. I knew I HAD to become "somebody" real soon.

One of my well-meaning "aunts" said, "Yvette is gonna end up like Olivia. She likes walking the streets too much."

Oh my God, that statement hurt me to the core. I heard it repeatedly like reverb in my psyche for years, even decades. Why would anyone say that to someone - especially a child? Olivia was the girl in the song by The Whispers entitled "Lost and Turned Out". The lyrics said Olivia got distracted by a wolf in lamb's clothes on the way to her grandmother's. The wolf led her astray and she was lost and turned out. Olivia the slave, was lost and turned out like 10 million girls in the world. Olivia, Olivia, Olivia.

Being raised in the church, those lyrics and that "aunt's" words seemed prophetic. Everything my grandmother told me was there: 1) the devil was lurking around, out to get me 2) the opportunity to break her heart and 3) to get lost in THIS world. Oh yes, I would be hell-bound for sure. That revelation ended my hood-hiking excursions immediately. After school activities and practices were 86'd – ended - done! During that time street walking prostitutes and pimps were visible fixtures in my community. I didn't want to be the next person lured or abducted into the lifestyle. My life became very, very linear - school, church and home sitting next to my grandmother. I told myself I was keeping me "in-place" because I didn't want to worry her. The truth is, as crazy as it sounds, I didn't want the "devil" to get me. It didn't help my paranoia seeing the number of street ministers with hand-made poster signs in big bold black letters and bull horns forecasting the end of the world on every corner.

Well, I made it through high school. Many of the senior activities I didn't participate in for a variety of reasons; primarily because I was SO ready to move forward and onward. With a couple of partial scholarships in the bag I was headed to the University of Miami! WooHoo! Other than location, I really didn't know where I was going. I liked the notion that I was in motion. The "buts" started butting in. And, guess what joined this penchant parade of thoughts. ALL those unanswered questions I had harbored since the beginning of time. The song "Theme from Mahogany" by Diana Ross captured those questions. How could she know what I was feeling? Those lyrics rang in my spirit.

> DO YOU KNOW WHERE YOU'RE GOING TO?
> DO YOU LIKE THE THINGS THAT LIFE IS SHOWING YOU,
> WHERE ARE YOU GOING TO?
> DO YOU KNOW...?

***

My time at the University of Miami was short and embarrassing. I was overwhelmed and underprepared for EVERYTHING. As the idiom goes, I was as lost as a goose in a windstorm. I packed my things and headed back to Liberty City. It took me nearly seven years to heal from the self-embossed capital "L" I felt was embedded like a crown of thorns in my heart and on my forehead. I failed big time.

The healing process began in the most unconventional way. I remember that night clearly. I was working the midnight shift at a hotel. I began to cry profusely. I couldn't believe my life had gotten so off-track. I said a very simple prayer: "Lord help me please."

Suddenly, I heard someone scream, "Hey You! Get yourself together and start your new life now!"

It startled me. Then I lifted my eyes toward the sound and it was an infomercial for a career college. The closing statement was, "So are you gonna just sit there or are you gonna make that choice today?" As soon as my shift ended at 7:00am, I drove approximately 15 miles to the Art Institute of Ft. Lauderdale. I sat in the parking lot shaking and crying waiting for the office to open.

When I mustered the courage to walk into the building the entire process was "user -friendly". Everything was looking up again for me. I felt at home. Everyone was like me; someone that needed that extra boost to navigate

an environment that was unfamiliar. Many of my peers were first generation collegians, single parents, ex-convicts, displaced workers, second
career seekers, late bloomers, etc. I call "US" - NON-TRADITIONAL. Most
did not transition directly from high school to a post-secondary education.
Because I was successful in another institution of higher learning I was
finally able to say I have a college degree.

I took the graduation ceremony personally. The rousing applause and cel-
ebratory shout-outs was a balm to my ailing spirit. I felt I had ingratiated
myself to humanity. I knew at that moment I wanted to be an instructor
for the non-traditional population. I found myself. I am them and they are
me. I can't live up to the unreasonable expectations and life scripts others
have laid-out for me. Nor do I want to anymore. There is room at the cross
for everyone, including people like me. So, who am I? I am the "certain
woman".

I didn't come from pedigree. Everything about my upbringing suggested
that I shouldn't and wouldn't make it in life. And everything prior to my
"nontraditional" matriculation said I couldn't. But GOD, reminded me that
I was accepted in the beloved. That I don't need a title. I don't need a particular background. In fact, I don't need a big-time name for Him to know me
and bless me. Throughout the Bible we see several accounts of Jesus with
a "certain woman". And, in every interaction that "certain woman" was a
much better person AFTER she spent a moment with Jesus.

I am the Certain Woman in Judges 9:53 who was bold enough to address a
power-struck ministry leader that was oppressing the flock. While everyone else was cornered in fear in a tower this "certain woman" brought
Gideon's son Abimelek's reign of terror unceremoniously to an end. I am
not the person that will blindly follow someone just because of their title.
Not only was I raised in the church, the Word of God was inoculated into
every fiber of my being. I found Him to be Jehovah-Sabaoth, the Lord my
Protector.

I am the Certain Woman in 2 Kings 4:1 that has had severe money challenges.
Nearly every financial upset one can face in this world I have experienced:
evictions, car repossessions, unemployment, judgments, foreclosures, etc.
Through all those hard times I learned financial prudence and sensibility.

I learned to trust the LORD more and more. I also learned and continue to learn He is Jehovah-Jireh, the Lord my provider.

I am the Certain Woman in Mark 5:25 that had battles with a potpourri of medical conditions. I've had my hip dislocated, an impinged shoulder, and acute gastritis to name a few. Health crises can be debilitating and have a domino effect on your overall livelihood. Even if you have insurance, doctors' visits, prescriptions and medical supplies are costly. Not to mention your limited ability to pay your bills and take care of your family if the illness lasts longer than your employer's sick leave. But through it ALL, I learned He is Jehovah-Rophe, the LORD that heals thee.

I am the Certain Woman in Luke 11:27 that will lift my voice and praise Him. I know Who brought me from 62nd Street and 14th Avenue in the Pork & Beans projects, to this present day. I love and appreciate my Liberty City upbringing. I love it all: the food, the styles, the sights and sounds. Especially the sounds! There's nothing like it; Uncle Luke and the Miami Bass, Gloria Estefan and the Miami Sound Machine, Pastor Marc Cooper and the Miami Mass Choir, to name a few. I learned through my insecurities of not fitting in, that my identity is with divinity. I may never be a part of the "in-crowd" and I am perfectly fine with that. I learned HE is Jehovah Tsidkenu, the LORD my righteousness.

The song "He Still Loves Me" from The Fighting Temptations movie soundtrack resonates in my heart and adequately expresses my life. Like the song says, "I want to make it crystal clear, that it took me a while, I am finally here. I was picked on, picked out, beat down, friends talked about me and even though I may not be good enough, God still loves me."

The aforementioned occurrences were in the late 1980's and early 1990's. Since then, I have graduated Summa Cum Laude with a Master of Science degree in Criminal Justice and a Doctorate of Education in Pastoral Community Counseling. I have kept my promise to the LORD and myself to reach out to "non-traditional" populations. I know what it's like to have people preaching your eulogy before you have had the opportunity to live.

At one post-secondary institution where I taught, I had a young lady who would wear heels and shorts to class. She was very defensive and full of sassiness. Many on the staff spoke negatively about her and my superiors began to chide me for not reprimanding her behavior, dress code, etc. I pointed out that she was never late to class, always had her homework completed, she participated meaningfully during class discussion and, lastly her "behavior" was not directed towards anyone.

I asked them, "Have you ever thought that her "attitude" was all she had left?" I asked them to give the little girl a break.

One day when she realized the searing eyes were no longer as prevalent she asked me, "Why was I the only person that was always so kind to her?" When I looked at this young lady, I saw my "old self" looking back at me. It was all I could do not to burst into tears.

I said to her, "I am going to answer your question with a question. YOU tell me why you don't deserve someone being nice to you?" I could see the walls she had built around her heart crumble.

She looked at me in the feeblest way and asked faintly; "I do?"

I answered back affirmatively, "YOU DO!" When I saw her again years later, I didn't recognize her. She gave me a hearty hug and reminded me of that encounter. Praise the LORD, this little tightly woven rosebud had blossomed into a beautiful flower.

I felt like I was really walking in my calling. Everything was falling in place. I was living "the dream" and it felt SO good. The thought that the LORD could use me to make a positive difference in someone's life prompted me to pursue Christ more and more. My earnest prayer became Philippians 3:10; that I may know Him, and the power of His resurrection, and the fellowship of His sufferings. Well, well, well, as the adage goes, be careful what you pray for. Pardon my colloquialism but in a matter of seconds, after I said "Amen" - or so it seemed - I went from being "on top of the world" to the "world being on top of me". I prayed and cried to the LORD for an explanation. While He doesn't have to confirm anything, in His lovingkindness He sent a message to me through my former first lady, the late Minister Marsha Screen of New Vision for Christ Ministries in Miami.

I remember it as if it was yesterday. Minister Marsha prophesied that the LORD was moving me. "Sister Rowland," she said. "You are growing fast. The LORD has put so much into you and He wants to use you. He's going to send you to places where people don't know the LORD the way you do."

Oh Lord! I was NOT excited! I loved (and still love) Miami. I NEVER wanted to leave home. But, what an experience it has been. Nothing prepared me for people problems in the house of the Lord. Those old feelings of not being what others THINK I should be started all over again. People were confronting me every other minute about my Miami style of dressing and behaving. I was so hurt, disappointed and offended. This welcoming was NOT the Southern hospitality I read about in cooking magazines. Some had the audacity to accuse me of all types of activities that I have never thought about doing: club hopping, adultery, getting high, etc. It had gotten so bad I was afraid to go to church for the first time in my life. I literally cried out to the LORD and asked Him why He would send me somewhere to be treated SO badly. I reached out to my Minister Marsha. Her voice was loving and soothing, but her words were stern and solid. She said I needed to get rid of that fear and ended the conversation with prayer.

Fear? I kept thinking, 'I'm not afraid of anyone.' I was earnestly praying that I wouldn't have to physically defend myself one day. The confrontations were getting just that bold and more frequent. After much prayer and fasting, the Lord showed me that I feared their faces, their scowls, sneers and the disapproving body language of someone who was different from them . That was a turning point. I was no longer enduring this assignment from the LORD. I remembered WHO I was. I am that "certain woman" who Jesus loves with an everlasting love. All the "certain women" in the Bible were in unchartered waters when Jesus ministered to them. On many occasions, He commended them on their faith in bringing the matter to Him. I learned, once again, God didn't call me to be popular, or to be accepted in the "who's who" circle. Moreover, on a multiplicity of occasions the disciples didn't recognize Jesus. Therefore, I shouldn't have been alarmed that "church people" were rejecting me.

I also learned not to take rejection personal in my professional life. Prior to moving to Texas, I had earned multiple awards for my work with non-traditional populations. I was very happy and looked forward to being a campus director one day. That was my career path. Well, that dream quickly started looking like a nightmare. At one post-secondary institution I had one student that hated me. Worst of all, that individual partnered with some co-workers to sabotage my class and credentials. Every day it was one shenanigan after the next. I couldn't believe professionals could be so cruel and deceitful. Instead of feeding into the toxic unorthodox relationship, I made up my mind to stay focused on my purpose. I decided not to allow this student to be a distraction to me or the other students. The more I stabilized my emotions, the stronger I became. One day I looked up from my desk and realized I had attained peace in the midst of confusion. I honestly don't know when I became mute to the drama. I do know that my resolve to be used by the LORD is much more powerful than being popular with the masses. I DO NOT love, like or want the glory that comes from man more than the glory that comes from God (John 12:43).

***

I taught for three years at one of the state male prison facilities in Texas. I loved every minute. My class was mandated for 26-weeks to prepare them for the parole board. My ambition was to assure them that they were precious in the eyes of the LORD. I wanted them to know that our God is a God of many chances. I wanted them to have a positive classroom experience to empower them to continue their education.

It bothers me when someone says school isn't for everyone. IT ABSO-LUTELY IS! It's the culture of the institution and the teaching style of the instructor that may not be congruent with that individual's temperament.

In class one day an inmate said to me, "Doc, I didn't know they had women like you in the world. I've been in and out of jail for the past eight years. Now I feel like I can really make something of myself."

I asked, "What do you mean "women like me"?

He responded, "You know ... I used to think it was only one way to make it in this life and you showed me it's not too late. Man, you understand how it feels when people try to make you feel worthless." In my heart I knew all too well that grievous sentiment.

The biggest lesson of all is the revelation that everything I experienced was custom designed by God to mature me in all areas of my life: mental, emotional and spiritual. From a little girl worshipping at the Historical Mt. Zion Baptist Church in Miami, Florida to a middle-aged woman praising the Lord at Christian House of Prayer in Killeen, Texas. I KNOW that ALL things have indeed worked (are still working) together for my good. I love God. I love my Pastors Bishop Nate Holcomb and Pastor Valerie Holcomb. Being a part of their ministry has developed me in ways that have made me a much better person. Throughout Holy Writ many men and women of God were moved from their homeland (Genesis 12:1 & 2 Corinthians 6:17) for the LORD to mold them into mature servants.

> PSALM 139:14
>
> I WILL praise thee;
> for I am fearfully and
> wonderfully made:
> marvelous are thy works;
> and that my soul knoweth
> right well.

If you have experienced church hurt, rejection, inappropriate labeling, people problems and pain be encouraged by the scriptural affirmations that walked me through the hardest part of that journey:

> "We will NOT forsake the assembling of ourselves together, as the manner of some is; but exhorting one another: and so much the more, as ye see the day approaching." (HEBREWS 10:25)

> "We ARE His workmanship, created in Christ Jesus unto good works, which God hath before ordained that we should walk in them." (EPHESIANS 2:10).

> "We ARE a chosen generation, a royal priesthood, a holy nation, a peculiar people; that ye should shew forth the praises of him who hath called you out of darkness into his marvelous light." (1 PETER 2:9)

"I WILL praise thee; for I am fearfully and wonderfully made: marvelous are thy works; and that my soul knoweth right well." (PSALM 139:14)

"And He hath put a new song in my mouth, even praise unto our God: many shall see it, and fear, and shall trust in the LORD." (PSALM 40:3).

"...and He said unto me, My grace is sufficient for thee: for My strength is made perfect in weakness. Most gladly therefore will I rather glory in my infirmities, that the power of Christ may rest upon me." (2 CORINTHIANS 12:9).

Yes, even me.

YVETTE'S PRAYER

My loving caring sharing Heavenly Father,

With Your very own hands You formed me. I thank You for breathing Your wisdom over me, so I can understand Your purpose for my life.

I thank You for Your continual protection. When they see me waiting, expecting Your Word, those who reverence You will take heart and rejoice with me.

I can see now, GOD, that Your decisions are right; Your testing has taught me what's true and right.

Oh, thank You for loving me—ALWAYS— and holding me tight just the way You promised.

Lord You comfort me in my sad days, so I can live, I mean really live.

Your revelation of Who I am is the tune I dance to.

Despite all the tricks and schemes that satan used by sending people to be hurtful, I will keep my mind fixed on Your counsel.

In Jesus Name, Amen

Scriptural Interlude

For I was an hungred, and ye gave me meat: I was thirsty, and ye gave me drink: I was a stranger, and ye took me in: Naked, and ye clothed me: I was sick, and ye visited me: I was in prison, and ye came unto me.

MATTHEW 25: 35-36

Well reported of for good works; if she have brought up children, if she have lodged strangers, if she have washed the saints' feet, if she have relieved the afflicted, if she have diligently followed every good work.1 Timothy 5:10 having a reputation for good works; and if she has brought up children, if she has shown hospitality to strangers, if she has washed the saints' feet, if she has assisted those in distress, and if she has devoted herself to every good work.

FIRST TIMOTHY 5:10

For even the Son of man came not to be ministered unto, but to minister, and to give his life a ransom for many.

MARK 10:45

The Divine Assignment for My Life

By: Crystal Lee

I am sure I looked like someone hired to work in a highly specialized laboratory experiment. I had to wear protective clothing. I was covered from top to bottom, gloves, paper shoes, paper bonnet and face shield. This was my first encounter caring for a person living with HIV/AIDS.

I was assigned as a Private Nurse at Miami's Jackson Memorial Hospital. I was not informed of the patient's diagnosis before I arrived. When I arrived, I was informed that the patient was in isolation because of his AIDS-related

> ## ISAIAH 41:4 KJV
>
> Who hath wrought and done it, calling the generations from the beginning? I the Lord, the first, and with the last; I am he.

illness diagnosis. I was provided a report on the isolation techniques that would have to be used to care for him. I felt like a character from a science fiction movie.

He was a young married man from Peru; he was admitted complaining of severe headaches and visual changes. I introduced myself; but, he only spoke Spanish, so our communication was verbally limited. I met his immediate needs; assisting with all his daily living activities.

His family probably wondered why I was always dressed in the isolation garments. I realized after taking care of this young man, who always looked so bewildered and sad, when his family came to visit; that he had not disclosed his diagnosis with them. His family would embrace him and kiss him. His wife would lie next to him in the bed and cuddle with him at times. I was concerned about the risk that this rare disorder posed for the patient's family. The doctors were permitted to disclose his diagnosis to his family with his permission. His wife would need to be tested for the HIV virus; it was probably the reason for his sadness knowing that he would have to tell her. He had an AIDS defining diagnosis, yet his wife was still at risk of being HIV positive.

The Lord provided with me compassion for this patient from Peru and allowed me to provide the most humane and professional care that my nursing experience had taught.

I believe in Divine intervention and assignments for our lives. God created each of us with a role for the world that He created. I became a Licensed Practical Nurse in February 1977; my assignments were usually in specialty areas. I worked Geriatrics, Prison Medicine, Labor and Delivery, Pediatrics and for the last 27 years (as of 2018) HIV/AIDS.

My mother was my inspiration for becoming a nurse. She decided one day to change the course of her life. She attended Lindsey Hopkins Adult Education Center in Miami and graduated a year later. She went on to take the Florida State Board of Nursing exam passing with a high score. Through this first encounter with an HIV patient; I believe that God planted a seed in my heart to become an instrument and an extension of His unconditional love for people living with this medical condition. God gave me an understanding that HIV/AIDS does not discriminate; if the risk factors are present anyone, even I can be infected. The medical community initially identified the cases among the gay population; IV drug users due to sharing their works (needles) and sex workers. As time went on pregnant women, married people and persons that were in monogamous relationships were being infected.

I had a burning desire to learn more about this disorder and I started reading articles and attending trainings provided by the Florida Department of Health. I needed to be equipped to care for persons living with this incurable virus, originally called GRID (Gay Related Immune Deficiency Syndrome).

I enlisted in God's army to educate by sharing the prevention message that I was trained to disseminate. I would fight against the battle of discrimination; stigma, isolation and rejection of persons living with GRID; that would later come to be known as HIV/AIDS.

My enlistment came through a two-day training in June 1990. The Title of the Educational Program was HIV Counseling; Testing and Partner Elicitation Course. Lori Jordahl MBA-HA, CHE, Coordinator HIV Counseling and Testing, was a part God's plan in equipping me for this sensitive, yet great assignment. Lori continues to be highly respected in the HIV/AIDS Arena.

Lori made a statement that floored me. She said, "Every time you have unprotected sex with a partner, you are literally sleeping with everyone that he or she has slept with for the last 10 years."

It was a wakeup call for me and I was afraid that I might have acquired the virus. I did not have any conversations with my intimate partners about their sexual history. I marched my scared self to the Health Department and took the test. It was the longest two weeks of my life waiting for the test result to come back. The testing counselor called me and scheduled an appointment for me to receive my test results. I arrived at the clinic early. The counselor made several statements and the way he spoke I thought that I was positive for HIV. He informed me - finally - that the results were negative and presented me with a copy of the results. He provided me with a bag of condoms and wished me the best.

I had been spared by the grace of God from acquiring the virus and I wanted to educate others about safe sex and HIV/AIDS prevention. I gained more knowledge about the disease process; modes of transmission and the available treatments and ongoing research to find a cure.

I became a volunteer HIV/AIDS Educator, tester and counselor in my community. I was sad whenever I had to give a positive test result in the beginning. God gave me resolve. It was better for the person to know the results of their HIV status, so that they could get treatment. Not knowing or ignoring the test results could lead to advanced HIV or AIDS. God has empowered me and given me a boldness to address the people in any venue that He sends me to receive lifesaving information.

HIV/AIDS was very personal for me and my family. My brother is an openly a gay man. He began to present with some symptoms of GRID. My mother was suspicious and feared that my brother had acquired the virus. Like so many, during that time, he denied that he was infected with HIV for many years. He continued to live his life as if nothing had changed, although we saw that drastic changes in his health. We encouraged him to get tested; confide in us and to seek medical treatment. He was left with the reassurance that we loved him unconditionally and supported him regardless of his HIV status.

My brother visited my mom and during that visit she found some of his medication hidden in his belongings. My mom's greatest fear was confirmed. She confronted him about the medication and he denied that the medication was treatment of AIDS. My brother, like many others, was dying in denial, for fear of rejection, judgment and condemnation. We respected his right to disclose his HIV status when he was ready.

Finally, the call came from my brother. He was ready to talk about his status. "The doctor said that I have HIV." He later disclosed that his T-Cell was 0.5; a normal T-Cell count was 700 to 1500 according to the lab processing the test. My brother shared that he had several other sexually-transmitted diseases, as well as, Kaposi Sarcoma (an AIDS-related cancer), and tuberculosis. My brother needed our support more than ever before; but he was living alone in New York. My mom began to visit him twice a year. We arranged for him to come to Miami two other times each year to spend time with the family.

The positive side of my brother finally disclosing his HIV/AIDS status is that he sought treatment for AIDS at the Manhattan New York's VA Hospital. A US Navy veteran with an Honorable Discharge meant he was entitled to all military benefits including medical care.

I was resolved to give each person that I encountered living with HIV/AIDS the compassion, respect, consideration and love that we desired for my brother. It was clear to us that once he felt accepted and loved by his family - regardless of his sexual preference or HIV status, with treatment he began to heal. Donald has received the best care afforded him and today he is healthy with a 500 T-Cell count and his viral load is undetectable, which is the optimal God (next to complete healing) for anyone living with the virus. Amen

He has medical conditions related to genetics and side effects related to his medications. The Medical Staff at Manhattan' New York VA Hospital continue to provide excellent care and service to my beloved brother.

During my time of educating and assuring that Donald was fighting with his army of family behind him, I was looking for a new church home. I attended the first service that New Birth Baptist Church, now one of South Florida's most prominent churches, at Miami Northwestern Senior High School. I remember the date clearly - June 16, 1991. It was prophesized in a letter I received from Televangelist Robert Tilton June 11, 1991; that I would be led to a new church and the Holy Spirit would be in operation and the word of God would be taught and preached effectively. The letter advised that I was not to be hearer only of the word. It encouraged me to join at least one ministry and to become active in that ministry. As of this writing, 27 years later, I am still actively participating in ministry and honoring the prophesy.

God had prepared me for this area of nursing; I do it so those receiving care know that God loves them regardless of their diagnosis or how they contracted the disorder. My former administrator, the Head Nurse in the Ambulatory Care Center at Jackson Memorial Hospital, was opening a new HIV/AIDS Clinic and offered me a position in SID Clinic (Special Immunology Corridor D). I accepted the offer and was the first nurse hired for the clinic. Our clinic was like a one stop service clinic, meeting most of their needs without going to other places in the hospital.

I received an eight-week orientation and training that enhanced my nursing skills and I acquired new skills. I was excited and loved working with our patients. I came to work anticipating that I would make someone's life better.

Initially our patient population was gay men. It was the role of the staff, including the Special Immunologists to make our clients feel special. The clients received superior medical care in the clinic and received referrals to necessary providers or other specialty services as needed. It was a place to gather and socialize with persons sharing things in common, at the same time receiving medical services. The patients were respected. They could be themselves without fear of rejection or condemnation and that was critical in assuring that they were open to treatment and felt comfortable to ask every question they needed to. As time went on we saw a shift in our patient population; there was an increase in non-homosexual or gay persons attending the clinic. We saw more women attend the clinic, and the patients' ages also changed. There were older men and women that were diagnosed HIV-positive receiving care.

I was gainfully employed as a Licensed Practical Nurse II. I believe that everything in my life was being coordinated in the spirit realm and I had absolutely nothing to do with it. I say that because on 1992, I was approached by Elder George Fishburne at the church I was attending (New Birth Baptist). He asked if I would consider becoming the Coordinator of the Healing Hands Ministry of the church. I sought God for direction and accepted the assignment. I began to solicit members to join the ministry. Members came and left because they were concerned about confidentiality if they disclosed their HIV/AIDS status with the group. We were there to serve though, and it was made clear to everyone in that ministry, that confidentiality was required and critical. If anyone discussed what goes on in the ministry, it would have to be with the person's permission or there was nothing to talk about.

I remember a former member requested that we move our monthly meetings to the church's human services building away from the main church building. She wanted to be a part of the Healing Hands Ministry but did not want anyone to think that she was HIV positive. We shifted our meeting to accommodate her and she never attended one meeting at the new meeting site. I was disappointed, but God taught an important lesson, you cannot serve those whom you are afraid to touch and afraid to relate to.

I met and still meet challenges in church setting. I have had limitations imposed when I was providing education to the Body of Christ. I did not give up and continued to educate others on HIV Prevention. I believe that God anoints us to do what He has assigned for us to do. While some limitations became closed doors, because of the need and concern; and because of God's hand, I have been allowed to address other churches in the community and the information and supplies were received with eagerness. God's healing will go forth beyond pews, beyond limitations, beyond fears and beyond stigmas.

Dr. Juanita Conward, and other New Birth Baptist Church Trustees, wrote a grant for and HIV/AIDS prevention program for youth called "The Buddy Project." The kids were from the community-at-large, diverse in cultural backgrounds and came from several different schools. The ages of the kids were 12 to 18 years old. The program's participants were instrumental in educating over 3,000 persons in Miami-Dade County on HIV Prevention. They spoke at schools, churches and outpatient substance abuse programs.

My journey while working in the HIV/AIDS Arena has presented many challenges and some defeats; yet I stand on the word of God, I can do all things through Christ, who strengthens me. I thank God for foreword thinking church leaders like Bishop Victor Curry. In his capacity as President and General Manager of South Florida gospel station AM 1490 WMBM, he presented me with his vision for Compassion Talk Show. It was a platform to discuss openly discuss HIV/AIDS in communities of color, and congregations during the early 2000s. The vision, I believe came after a conference call that must have been God orchestrated. Several prominent pastors were on the call and heeded the charge to act against an incurable disorder that was claiming the lives of people in their congregations at alarming rates. They each implemented an action plan in their ministries in different states.

The Body of Christ needs to have a level of comfort discussing all medical conditions. Part of this happens as information is disseminated through qualified medical professionals. Most churches have Health Ministries with members who are doctors, nurses and other healthcare staff. It is through those professionals willing to serve in ministry capacities that our communities – those in the pews and chairs – can win the battle against not only HIV/AIDS but obesity, diabetes, hypertension and other illnesses. God has placed healers in the Body of Christ; and leaders must allow them more liberty in ministering to those who need it most.

> **JOHN 1: 2**
>
> Beloved, I pray that you may prosper in all things and be in health, just as your soul prospers.

For Third John 1: 2 says, "Beloved, I pray that you may prosper in all things and be in health, just as your soul prospers." The men and women called of God to preach and teach The Word of have an obligation to share the word of God without prejudice; condemnation and or bias. That same thing must hold true when it comes to ministering to those with HIV/AIDS, addiction problems or other sexually-related illnesses. I remember when babies were being born HIV positive to mothers that were HIV positive and the mother did not get prenatal care. It would break my heart. The law began to require that pregnant women get tested for STDS at the initial pregnancy diagnosis and in the third trimester of the pregnancy. I am proud to say – and all of us on the HIV/AIDS battlefield were rejoicing – that in Miami-Dade County, Florida, only one baby was born HIV positive in 2017. While we rejoiced, we still fight and educate, because it is the goal of the medical community that "not one more baby be born HIV positive."

God has used my nursing skills to assist others with an array of medical conditions. I am not limited to just serving those living with HIV/AIDS. I provide the same compassionate love and care to those in need, whether the diagnosis is cancer; diabetes, kidney failure, heart disease, respiratory disorders - it is all part of the Ministry of Nursing. I believe that God orders my steps toward the person that needs the nursing skills that I am capable of providing.

There have been so many advances in the medical arena; there is new found hope for treatment of every disease and disorder. Medical scientists have developed a cure for Hepatitis C. Truvada which is known as a PrEP (Pre-exposure prophylaxis) is now used to prevent a spouse or intimate partner from contracting HIV from an infected person.

Every day of my life on this side eternity was designed and orchestrated by my heavenly Father before the foundation of the world. My parents were supposed to meet, get married and be intimate with each other, so that all 10 (yes, 10) of us would be conceived and born for a special assignment in God's plan.

Every gift that He has entrusted me with - God will get the glory and honor. I thankful to Him for sending me into a vineyard of people needing love and understanding. I am grateful and honored that God uses me to talk to and share condoms with the young prostitute that stands on the corner selling her body. The young men that never had a father and they are looking for acceptance. These young men may join gangs or participate in other illegal activities. And somehow, God leads me to them. They are my children – my assignments of compassion.

I distribute condoms in some of the communities in South Florida, primarily in predominantly lower socioeconomic communities sprinkled with drug sales, prostitution and gun violence. Two of those areas are known as Liberty City and Brownsville, communities within the incorporated Miami and Miami-Dade County. There must be hundreds of churches in those two years alone. Often, as I am doing "ministry" there, I wonder how many times these men or women of God have tried to approach the lost souls surrounding their sanctuaries and find out how the church can assist them. Do you ever wonder why young men are sitting on bus stops or standing on corners with their flesh exposed as cars pass? Many have experienced an abusive childhood episode; and it was not addressed or shared with anyone. Maybe encountering them sincerely and intimately, the way we should encounter Christ will help them receive healing. One real conversation or gesture may change the way they view or value themselves. I have witnessed young MEN prostituting themselves on those very corners putting their bodies and lives in dangers. I pray for them as I drive through the streets of our community.

The church is often called a spiritual hospital. We are to share God's unconditional love and understanding without being judgmental. Our purpose is to love others, as God so loves us and to minister to the spirit and soul of people, just as medical doctors provide care for the physical body.

I had a 94-year-old widow I was blessed to care for. Her husband never disclosed his HIV status to her. She would tell me the story of how she met him. Oh, how she would smile every time she talked about him and that meeting. She loved him, as much as she did the day they met. She was not angry with her husband for transmitting the HIV virus to her. Somehow, she found comfort in loving the man she had known all those years.

I recall working with a young mom with five beautiful children. No matter how much support, services and counseling she was given; she absolutely refused to take her medication, keep her dialysis appointments or adhere to the doctor's orders. She gave up her two youngest kids for adoption - to one her neighbors. I was heartbroken when she gave up the younger kids. She relocated with her three teenage daughters to another part of Florida to be close to her family. She died shortly after relocating, leaving her three teenage daughters in the care of her family members. I believe that God welcomed her home to be with Him. She was a good mother to her children and prepared them for her death before she left this world.

My co-worker Patrick and I went to visit one of his patients at Jackson Memorial Hospital. He translated as I was led to pray for this patient during the visit. While I always prayed for clients, I was always encouraged when I could do so openly or was asked to pray. This patient had never disclosed her HIV status to her children for fear of rejection. She went home to be with the Lord two days later; because she was a Christian I believe she is in the presence of God today.

God is so wise and loving, that what He equips us to do for those outside of home; He also used at home. That was my blessing. I was equipped to provide care for my mother for 16 years. She was diagnosed with diabetes, crippling arthritis, glaucoma and Alzheimer's Disorder. While caring for her, we relocated her brother from Winter Gardens, Florida. Diagnosed with moderate retardation, mom was his Health Care Proxy; and as life would have it, I stepped into that role for both. Thankfully, my mother and uncle lived in the same senior citizen apartment building and it made easier to care for them. I was still working full time at Jackson Memorial Hospital while caring for my parents and uncle. My dad was diagnosed with cardiac issues and Schizophrenia Chronic Paranoid Type. He wasn't able to live alone any longer, and so he lived with me for three months until my nephew was able to find a facility 10 minutes from my home. God gave me grace for that caretaker's assignment through my years of nursing ministry. It wasn't easy, but it was easier because God walked the journey with me. He gave me peace of mind and the physical strength to keep going, and encouragement when I want to throw in the towel. My father, mother and uncle all transitioned, and I believe are in the presence of the Creator. I thank God for allowing me to be a part of so many of the lives of His people. Through His hands on me, I gave my skills to Him for the providing of compassionate care and love to them according to His Divine assignment for my life. I am grateful for the opportunity to be used by God outside the walls of the church. It is my passion to reach the disenfranchised and the hopeless, telling them that God loves them right now and will do so always.

CRYSTAL'S PRAYER

Father God in the name of Jesus Christ,

I ask that You revive and infuse us the Body of Christ with a burning desire to win souls to Christ.

Empower us to come out of our comfort zones and send us into the vineyards. The harvest is truly plentiful, yet the laborers are few.

Lord; empower our hearts, minds and lips with soul winning words and under the anointing of God that people will receive the invitation to discipleship.

In Jesus name, I pray – Amen!

She Is Strong, But She Knows Her Weaknesses

TRICKA D. BROWN

I wanted to try something different and new. The other girls were talking about their sexual experiences and how pleasurable they were. That was it! Sex would solve it all. While the option was present, I knew deep down inside that I couldn't act upon anything with another girl. Something stopped me. It was boys who I had the problem with. With boys, I still had some type of control. I would say, "You like me, come to my house then." This one particular boy followed me like a little puppet. He thought he was using me, but I was really using him. My body, my terms. He was just one of the boys who I had

> ## ROMANS 7:23
>
> But I see another law in my members, warring against the law of my mind, and bringing me into captivity to the law of sin which is in my members.

seen in the neighborhood. You wanted to sleep me with. Okay. No big deal. But, what I was trying to make happen, never did. When he left, I was still a virgin.

One of my guy friends, who I hung out with frequently invited me to a block party in a city about 20 minutes from where we lived. I can't down play this relationship, he was someone who I cared for and truth be told we had history. I was comfortable with him and he was part of my life since the first day we met. So, me hanging out with him was nothing new. That's what I did. I enjoyed his company and hanging with the fellas. I wasn't familiar with the area, but because I wanted to hang out, I went with them. We were dressed and looking good.

You already knew by the cars we were riding in, that we were about that life. Music blasting, rims shining, teeth sparkling. If there was a camera, it was filming us. They decided to park their cars and get out. There was not a cloud in the sky. As we were walking through the crowd of people, we noticed all types of cars, playing music as people drove up and down the streets. We were there to have a good time and make our own statement. If you didn't know us before, you would know us afterwards.

As we continued walking, my guy friend told me, "We are going back to the car because something doesn't feel right." He told me to get in the back seat and stay low. Demanding my own way and thinking he was hiding something, I started drama with him. Then there was that look. That look stopped all of my attitude and led me to the back seat to do what he said. As we were driving, it seemed like the car was going so slow. He was turned around looking through the rear window and the driver watched the front. All hell broke loose.

"I'VE BEEN SHOT!" I screamed from the top of my lungs.

I started screaming for my mom. My guy friend began to ask me where, with anger in his voice. I can't imagine what he was thinking. Maybe he thought I was hit by one of the bullets from the gun he was firing above my head. Maybe it was the bullets coming towards us from those trying to take our lives. I didn't know. All I felt was that something hit me, and it burned. As he looked at me, there was no evidence of blood. He continued looking and it was the shell from the bullet that hit me in my eyebrow. We drove home safely with no harm to any of us. Yet, it reminded me that I was in a fight that I did not ask for and did not look for.

But, I had a purpose. Jeremiah 29:11 covered me as well. "For I know the thoughts that I think toward you, saith the Lord, thoughts of peace, and not of evil, to give you an expected end." Should I fight, or should I die? There comes a time in our life when we have to decide if fighting for our self is worth it or not. We all encounter obstacles that make us wonder, "If this is the one that will take me out?"

Depression is one such fight. It is the silent battle that we rarely speak about, but it mentally drains you and it leaves us vulnerable. We struggle with the simple things like getting out of the bed, answering the phone, grabbing something to eat or just showing up. What makes the battle with depression different from other battles we face is that it's not a fight against someone else, it's the fight within ourselves.

There were certain triggers in my life that made depression a serious challenge of mine. Some days it caused me to act as if I didn't care and on other days it brought about suicidal thoughts. "One day at a time", is what I would tell myself, not realizing that events in my life would cause me to live life moment by moment. From surviving sexual assault, to overcoming tragedies, to ducking from bullets that whisked by. It's in these moments of my life, that I knew I needed something or someone to save and rescue me from the course of life I was on.

It was just the three of us; my mom, brother and me, as my father was nowhere to be found. My mom was a hard worker, but not home as much as I wanted her to be. My brother on the other hand was tough and never showed much emotion. And then there was me. I was that girl! I was fatherless, skinny, light skinned with big lips and my hair was braided with beads. To top it all off, I had the silver metal braces on my teeth that were once very popular.

My time in elementary school was an awkward stage in life for me. I was trying to find out who I was and where I fit. On one particular day, I had allowed the kids in class to push me up to fight a boy. It was my first real fight. It would be nothing like fighting my brother because he knew he couldn't hurt me. Growing up, my mom and brother always told me, "If someone hits you, you hit them back." We learned, "If someone crossed the line, you defend yourself." I remembered the lessons I had been taught. I should have been scared to fight this boy, but I wasn't. He was taller and bigger than me, but I didn't care. I wasn't going to let anyone see me not stand up for myself. It was a short and quick fight, as the teacher stepped in and stopped it. When the principal called me in the office, my butt was not prepared for that paddle. I took it like a soldier though.

As time went on, my early teenage years were even more awkward. I entered middle school, and there was nothing cool about riding a big yellow bus. During the bus rides, we were judged based on where we were from. We had to defend ourselves against other kids because of where we lived. We had the occasional bus wars where we talked trash to kids on other buses, as we were determined to defend ourselves. Middle school was the one place that made me realize I did not look like the other girls I went to school with. They were beautiful, taller and I loved the way they dressed. I found myself admiring other girls that I could never end up being like, so I thought. Because of my deep and raspy voice, I would pray and ask God to change the way I sounded. It was in those instances, I knew He existed. Yet, I didn't feel I needed a relationship with Him. I just need Him to do some things for me from time to time. It was not a requirement in our house to attend church, so I did not make it a priority.

Middle school was the place where I learned that my lips could be used for other things. The boys would pick on me and they made sure I understood things about my lips. They would encourage me to perform oral sex on them, telling me since my lips were big; they knew I was good at it. If a boy liked me, I wasn't sure if it was because they knew what the other boys had said about me or if they liked me just for me. I was confused and ashamed. My outer appearance brought an insecurity to my inner self.

During some of our free time, the neighborhood kids and I would go to the pool. It was a fun place to hang out and cheap to get in. I knew I could not swim, but at least I could look cute. Just because I felt insecure on the inside, didn't mean everyone needed to know it. I would tell myself, I couldn't compete with the other girls. They had matured. My one-piece bathing suit did not compare to their two-piece bathing suits. While trying to build inner strength, it was clear to see that they had confidence and I lacked it. We are so much harder on ourselves than other people are. I wish someone had told me then, "Give yourself a break. Learn to love you. Learn to celebrate who you are."

One hot day as the sun was shining, we decided to go to the pool. It was close to where we lived, so it was no big deal to walk there. Even with my mom being strict, she would allow me to go to the pool with my friends from the neighborhood. When we got there, people were having fun as they laughed and played together. I felt happy and everything was good. I had no reason to be watchful or put my guard up. I did my norm; I stayed close to the wall and watched everyone do what they do. My friends got in and started swimming. As I was relaxing at the edge of the pool wall, one of the older boys grabbed my hands and began pulling me to the middle of the pool. I was so scared, but of course I was not going to show it. I started looking at him like he was crazy as he continued to pull me farther out in the water. With fear in my eyes, I told him to stop playing because I could not swim. The louder I got, the more he ignored me until he got me where he wanted me. With a smile on his face and laughter in his voice; fear overtook me, as he sexually assaulted me, touching me over and over again. He touched my breast, he touched my inner thighs, he touched the parts of me that had not been seen by another person.

Why is he doing this to me? I was confused and did not know whether I should be fighting being stuck in a place where I could not swim back to safety; or fighting the assault that I was enduring. While in this vulnerable place, the ultimate betrayal took place, as he tried to put his finger in my secret box. I used all the strength I could muster up to close my legs as tight as I could, while holding on for dear life. I couldn't believe this was actually happening to me, I didn't even know his name. This was one of the older boys; he should have been watching out for me. Nothing stopped his advances. Nobody noticed my distress. Nobody responded to my screams for help. Finally, after he had his way with me, he took me back to the wall of the pool.

To the natural eye I was back where I started, in a safe place within the pool, but my mind had shifted. I left the pool sad, lonely and depressed, with no words to say. I was once again ashamed and now a new kind of embarrassment gripped me. This situation forever changed and scarred me, and it caused me to stop wearing bathing suits completely. I realized the rules of the game had changed, but if you think you can hurt me and get away with it, you were wrong. An eye for an eye, as my heart harden.

Life continued, and I was living out a new normal. Trying to cover up what had happened, as if that day never transpired. However, it did happen and within myself, I knew it, no matter how much I tried to hide it. I didn't know who I could confide in, so I hid it within me.

One day, while my brother and I were home chilling, we heard a knock at the front door. As we opened the door, the man began to apologize to us for our loss. He went on to say, "I'm sorry your grandmother Iris has passed." My heart dropped! What was he talking about? My mom hadn't told us that she had passed away. I was struggling with her death. No one told us how sick she was. My mom said she didn't want the trauma of it all to affect us during the school week. I was angry with my mom. My grandmother was gone, and I wanted her back, I needed her here with me.

Before I knew it, we were burying the one who I thought knew me better than anyone. With her, I didn't have to protect myself or act like somebody I was not. Her beautiful brown skin, long hair and slender figure, in many ways she was part of me and I was part of her. Now she was gone. She was a special lady. I can see her now with a cigarette in her hand and her legs crossed. She loved and spoiled me. She was the first one who let me drive her car. Even when she was weak, she was strong.

After my grandmother's funeral, while we were all at the graveyard, I began to reminisce. My thoughts were everywhere. I had lost the person who made me feel safe and free. I didn't get a chance to say goodbye. She had left me with no warning and no explanation. My head was exploding. Something deep on the inside made me angry with everyone.

It happened so fast. All I remember was running. I ran, and ran, and ran until my aunt caught me. I don't know where I was running to, but I had to leave that place. Finally, as my aunt embraced me, I broke down and cried. I was broken. I don't know what she said, but she caught me as I was emotionally falling. As days went by, I felt familiar emotions reappear.

I had been a cheerleader both in elementary and in middle school. Cheering was the one thing that made me feel like I was part of something good. I wasn't being judged for my size or the neighborhood I was from. The more I practiced, the better I became. Even though cheering was nothing new for me, I had a new coach and she was different. She taught us to work hard, and she reminded us that we were one team.

Life had already taught me that I needed to build a wall around myself, don't trust anyone and to do everything I could to not reveal the girl within me. I did everything I could to hide the depression, betrayal, hurt, disappointment, grief, anger and bitterness until one day something happened, and I could no longer hide what was on the inside. Before I knew it, what was in me came out. "An eye for an eye, I'm a fighter."

If I felt any type of threat, I would hurt you before I let you hurt me. I would protect myself at all costs. The thoughts, pain, shame, and rage I had suppressed for so long took control! One word, one action and before I realized it, a bat was in my hand and I was ready to swing on another cheerleader. I could not stop myself! One thing for sure, that was everybody's warning, not to mess with me.

***

The girl in the mirror. I had forgotten what my mom had taught me. I had forgotten what I actually looked like. My insecurity had grown into something it never should have grown into. The secrets I had kept from my family had grown into something they should have never grown into. The things the boys said to me had changed me in ways they should never have. I failed to communicate to anyone that I was struggling in a battle on the inside of me. I had forgotten, but they had not forgotten me.

I ignored the fact that these emotions had access to my heart, mind and soul.

> ## JAMES 1:23-24 NIV
>
> Anyone who listens to the word but does not do what it says is like someone who looks at his face in a mirror and, after looking at himself, goes away and immediately forgets what he looks like.

I was young and had not acknowledged what I was dealing with. Although there was no visible evidence, I was crying on the inside and was unsure on how, or if I could make it through. I was tired. Maybe if the tears were showing on the outside my family would have noticed how much I had changed. The pain was eating me up. My grades in school started getting lower. My skin began to break out in rashes a physical manifestation of my internal turmoil. My experiences were tormenting me in the morning, afternoon and night. There was nowhere for this young girl to run or hide. It was as if the boogie man had found me. I wanted to die.

What was my purpose? Why did life hurt so bad? I continued to bury what was going on. Was I the blame for all that happened to me? Was this all my fault? Did I ask for it? Did I bring this on myself? You may think it's the fight with everyone else that destroys you, but it's the fight within yourself that you haven't let go that does the most damage.

I thought I was handling it. I know I wasn't. I only suppressed it. I was falling deeper into depression, needing to escape and wanting to get to a safe place, but I didn't know how. Girls and boys liked me, but truth be told, I didn't care. I was searching. If you wanted to talk, I would talk. If you wanted to hold my hand, then I would do that too. It didn't matter. I didn't care. I was looking for something to ease the pain. I started smoking weed, thinking that would mask my depression, but that just made me relax. I started drinking beer, thinking that would help, but it didn't do anything. Plus, I had gotten caught by my mom once. The disappointment in her eyes resonated so powerfully.

I continued my search for anything that would satisfy my pain. I continued fighting with my inner demons. Everything became a trigger. Loneliness even played a bigger role than expected so I tried my best to stay away from that. "….all the days of my appointed time will I wait, till my change come (Job 14:14)."

Then one day my life changed. I was invited to attend a family and friends church service. I didn't have any clothes that I believed were suitable for church. I was in between wearing daisy dukes shorts and other tight cloth-ing. All I could do was make sure I got there. As I look back on it now, there was no dress code for a lost soul, a broken spirit, a wondering vessel and a suicidal person. There was nothing anyone could do to me, to make me feel any worse than I already felt. Was I too lost to be found?

Sometimes you just need to make up your mind and just get there. Get to the altar. Get in prayer. Get somewhere that you know you can be honest and receive help. Just get there with what little strength you may have, and with whatever fight is left in you. This one decision can change your life. I had been to church a few times before, but this was one time being in church felt differently for me. I listened to every word that came out of the mouth of the people that were speaking. I didn't want to leave when the preacher started ministering. I came to church on that Sunday, broken into many pieces. My past had done a number on me and I came with no hope, no dreams, no wants and no desires. I had nothing in me, I was completely empty. I thought coming to church on empty was a bad thing, however, when I left that day I felt better than I had felt in a long time. I just kept going to church, not for people, but for me. I had decided to fight for me. I wanted to fight for me. Although I was vulnerable and weak, I still had a mind to want to fight for me. I couldn't fight for anyone else but me. If I was no good for me, I was no good for them. I was ready!

It was in the fight of my life. The thoughts of what I had been through still weighed me down, as if it was trying to exert power over me. The thoughts were still trying to control me. My mind would tell me not to trust anyone. It was like riding a never-ending roller coaster ride, because I would be happy one day and sad the next. It was those hidden things in my life: the mental anguish, the secrets, lies, the pretending I was good, when I really was not. They all were coming to the forefront the more I attended church.

One Sunday, as the service was ending, something was speaking to me. The preacher was offering salvation. "Get up and go!" the voice said. I sat in my shame and in my depression, I did not move. "Go," the voice said again.

I sat there pondering my pain. Although I had been going to church, I realized that I did not release any of the hurt, pain, disappointment and sadness that I had been dealing with. As benediction was done, I ignored what the voice said to me.

I started walking out of the church, when I heard it again, "Don't you leave until you give your life to Christ." I submitted to the voice.

I turned around and walked with my head down to where the preacher stood and said, "I have to give my life to Christ before I leave." Giving my life to Christ meant giving Him me and everything that was attached to me. My pain, my disappointments, my grief, my trouble, my sin. I laid it right there. "Here I am Lord, imperfect, not right, but I am here." I wanted Him to accept me with my messed-up self. I couldn't hide from Him because He was God. For the first time in a long time, I knew I had made a life changing decision.

I am more than what I've been through. Once I started thanking God for what I had gone through, the better I became in my mind. He didn't allow me to die on the day of the shooting. Even with my suicidal mindset, I didn't take the pills, nor did I drive myself off the road. He didn't allow me to drown in the pool. It was Him that allowed me to run at the graveyard, but not too far that I could not be reached. He kept me and spared my life from it all. I realized then that I had purpose.

Where ever you find yourself, know there is still hope and time for God to heal, deliver and set you free from whatever you are fighting. Shame and holding on to secrets will lead to the destruction of your inner self. It plays upon your mind and you begin to lose sense of reality. Whatever has occurred in your life thus far, I pray that you will allow God to be God. He is truly your strength.

The same sexual act performing, weed smoking, beer drinking, quick to fight girl has been used by God to pastor. I not only pastor because of the call on my life, I pastor because I love people. God can change and help anybody. It took Him to change me, in order for me to KNOW that He can change you. When it's all said and done, I AM A FIGHTER; I've just changed who and what I'm fighting for!

> **ISAIAH 53:5**
>
> "But He was wounded for our transgressions, He was bruised for our iniquities: the chastisement of our peace was upon Him; and with his stripes we are healed."

TRICKA'S PRAYER

Father,

As we come before your throne, acknowledging who you are; the God of our salvation, the King of Kings and the Lord of Lords. We come asking for your forgiveness for anything we have said or done in thy sight that was not pleasing to you.

I stand in the gap for anyone who is reading these words and may have lost their way. They may have forgotten that you are the only way. You are our refuge, a place where we can run and find safety.

You are the same God who protected, provided and love me unconditionally. I ask in the name of Jesus that you would wrap your arms around them and allow them to feel your touch.

According to Jeremiah 32:27, "Behold, I am the Lord, the God of all flesh: is there anything too hard for me?" Lord, the answer is NO! So, Father, I thank you in advance for the things that you will do in their lives from this day forward.

You have given them access to You and victory through You. You are Jehovah-Rapha, the God who heals, so we call on Your healing power, Your delivering power and the authority in heaven and in earth that You have.

Stand in the midst of every valley, every dark place, every dry place, every winter season, every place of rejection, anger, bitterness, shame, unforgiveness, loneliness, the very place in their lives that will cause them to not ask You for help or to trust in You. Cause their hearts to walk in forgiveness. Cause them to forgive the one that used them, the one that betrayed them and the one that did not love them. Cause them to understand that You have a way of working all things out for the good according to thy word.

 "And we know that all things work together for good to them that love God, to them who are the called according to His purpose." (Romans 8:28). Give them strength in this very hour and the days to come. Let the joy of the Lord be their strength (Nehemiah 8:10).

We say thank you!

We praise thy name!

We ask all these prayers in the name of Jesus.

Amen.

God Flipped the Script. My Life Has Never Been the Same

DEBRA WADLINGTON HOUSE

"This is it. It's about to change for you, Debra."

When I heard from God that morning, I ignored him. I never shall forget the day. Things did, in fact, change.

Four years later, when He gave me a prophetic word to deliver to the congregants in the church where I served as one the Associate Pastors, I began to experience what He had spoken that morning.

"Close the iPad Debra." I was in shock when God gave me a clear instruction not to take my iPad which held my well-written sermon on it to the pulpit for my time to preach. I always needed my manuscript to preach because my memory was bad; and it was really my crutch. I prayed for the ability to be able to preach without notes, but, I was never able to do it until the Sunday I delivered that prophetic message.

I took my iPad to the pulpit anyway and began to pray. I read my scripture and began my sermon titled "Let's Shift the Atmosphere." I was on a roll when God commanded that I close it and preach prophetically. I will never forget the looks and reaction I received. I was in awe; because I really was skeptical about the whole modern-day Prophecy Movement.

The message I delivered was a freeing one for all in attendance. God knew who would be there and who would receive it, and who would disseminate it via the gossip pool. He wanted us all to know that He was tired of us treating His temple like a drive through fast food restaurant. We walk in, place our order for what we need Him to do for us, put it in our bag, pay our bill and then drive back home and eat, or maybe just throw the meal in the trash. He was tired of His chosen ones treating His temple as a place where we get what we need - very quickly - so we can have the rest of my day to ourselves.

As I continued to read Second Chronicles 5:13-14 which was the scripture given to me by God to prepare my sermon, I could hardly speak. "It came even to pass, as the trumpeters and singers were as one, to make one sound to be heard in praising and thanking the Lord; and when they lifted up their voice with the trumpets and cymbals and instruments of music, and praised the Lord, saying, For he is good; for his mercy endureth for ever: that then the house was filled with a cloud, even the house of the Lord."

My voice weakened; but God's voice became as loud as the trumpets the verse talks about. As he changed my vocal chords to powerful and strong, I could not believe I was preaching without my notes. I could not believe I was preaching with conviction and not making the congregation feel good. I did not tell them to give their neighbor a high five, because God was telling them it was time to shift the atmosphere. It was not time out for judging and critiquing each other nor the preacher.

God demanded it was time for praising and lifting Him up in His temple. God declared in that message that He did not feel welcomed in His own temple because the focus of the worship service was no longer on Him but on the timing and traditions of the church. He let us know that the

Glory Cloud that filled the temple in the scripture could never come into the church, because it would not be recognized by the congregation. Their minds and hearts were tainted.

What poured out of me certainly shifted the atmosphere; and at that moment, I knew I would not be able to remain in that setting.

God had given me instructions to spread His gospel in a way that would draw His children that were lost, hopeless and in despair. These were those His Word spoke of in Matthew 25:35-40: "For I was an hungred, and ye gave me meat: I was thirsty, and ye gave me drink: I was a stranger, and ye took me in: Naked, and ye clothed me: I was sick, and ye visited me: I was in prison, and ye came unto me. Then shall the righteous answer him, saying, Lord, when saw we thee an hungred, and fed thee? or thirsty, and gave thee drink? When saw we thee a stranger, and took thee in? or naked, and clothed thee? Or when saw we thee sick, or in prison, and came unto thee? And the King shall answer and say unto them, Verily I say unto you, inasmuch as ye have done it unto one of the least of these my brethren, ye have done it unto me."

God wanted them to know He of His word, His goodness, His refuge, His grace and mercy. He wanted them to experience His glory, His peace and His comfort.

After this life changing experience, I never will ignore the knowledge and urgency of God's voice again. What God had predestined for me to carry out was manifesting. It became clear to me that things were never going to be the same. My new and ordained ministry journey was established. Everything I went through had a purpose. I was a Domestic Violence Survivor who had so much purpose behind my pain and I was ready to share my victorious testimonies of childhood molestation, teen pregnancy, being a teen wife and battles with depression and alcoholism.

I was raised in church and my first experience with childhood molestation happen there. I could not understand my mom's reaction when I told my her about what happened to me. Not only did she not console me, she told me to never tell that lie again. I was completely devastated; and I never wanted to hear about the goodness of Jesus again. I carried my secret and never shamed the family. Then, when I became a teenager it happened again, but that time I found a way to drown my pain in alcohol.

I was depressed; and I began to suffer from panic attacks. My family labeled my drunkenness as being a clown, the life of the party and felt I was quite entertaining. I, and my drunkenness, were a joke; so, no one thought to get me the help and care I needed.

I became involved with one of the preacher's sons and became a domestic violence victim, teenage mother and then a teenage wife. I was forced to marry because this was the proper thing to do. I had no marriage counseling, nor did anyone bother to ask if I wanted to live the rest of my life being beat up and mistreated. My mother was only concerned with not bringing anymore shame to the family. My father could not stop my mother's wishes because that's just what they did.

All that churching did nothing for my soul. My heart was broken, and my mind was sick. For the next ten years of my life I was beaten and raped by my husband. I was tied up and kept in a closet for days. I had two more children that I raised and provided for alone, even though we did not receive our divorce until the ten-year mark of our marriage. But there I was in the church, being a good wife and mother, living a lie and keeping everyone else happy and convinced that I was a good church member.

My church members knew what I was going through. I received no comfort or guidance from any of the church mothers or female leaders in the church. There were no female ministers I could go to. I felt I had no hope. I felt my mom had put the word out that I got what I deserved because of my sin of fornication, and that's why my pregnancy was cast upon me. God had to make me an example. I began to believe this as well.

I left that church after I married my second husband, my addiction uprooted, and I hit rock bottom numerous times.

I answered my call after I married my third husband. I was looking for love and could not find it. I relapsed and recovered multiple times but never wanted to do what God was calling me to do because I was hurt so bad in and at the church.

After, my third divorce, I began to surrender to God's call. I moved to Atlanta to start a new life. Chicago had given me enough drama and family disappointments, but I had to return to provide care for my sick father. Little did I know that my mom also needed my assistance. Even though I was doing well on my job, in the ministry I was serving at, and even at home, God made it very uncomfortable to stay in Atlanta.

I lost my job - due to bias. My ministry partners were not pleased with me because I was not COGIC (Church of God in Christ) and our Pastor allowed me to preach more often than they were asked. My best friend passed away. I struggled with deep depression and had panic attacks. At this time, I was sober, but I never went to therapy for alcoholism because I was a minister and was taught I only needed Jesus.

My father's health took a turn for the worst, so I had to leave Atlanta and return home. So back to Chicago I went. Back to the drama and pain. Back to the let downs and memories of abuse. Back to a state of confusion. Back to being the hero. Back to the cover ups.

My dad passed, and I went into a deeper depression. Then my mom was diagnosed with Dementia and my whole world was changed forever, at least that is what I thought. After dealing with the difficulty of grieving the loss of my dad and at the same time providing specialized care for my mom (which I found out the hard way I could not do it alone) and without professional help, I picked up the bottle once again.

I tried to stop drinking but I could not. I had rededicated my life back to my home church to make my dad proud. I felt I would feel closer to him if I went back to the church he loved so much. My dad never really prayed or studied the Bible in my presence. He loved God and his church. I realized, as I matured, most church members do the same. They have love for God (more for their church); but their love doesn't lead them to intimately pray or study the Word. This is why God is so upset, and that is why He gave me that prophetic word - to deliver and release me from the bondage of church walls.

I was different from the other ministers. Not only my appearance, but my entire demeanor was different form all of them. I did not wear fancy suits or pretty dresses. But I was so glad to be back in my home church after the 15 years of the second departure. I left the church the first time because I went back to the world where I felt I would be treated better. I had endured molestation and domestic violence at an early age and in my teen and young adult years from the hands of relatives who attended my church.

My church history was well known within the church. My pastoral team were all aware of my past experiences and they would often reflect on the negativity that engulfed my church history.

I thought my exposed alcoholism secret was causing my church members and pastoral team to treat me different, but then I heard God's voice again letting me know my release had come.

It was time for me to do what I was assigned to do when God called me to preach the Gospel.

It is my belief that God knew it would take something drastic to happen to me for me to move out of His way and do what He needed me to do because in my past I believed that because I was a Christian I had to endure all the pain that came my way because of my sins. It was my punishment. I did not know that God was a forgiving God. I did not understand what true repentance meant. I only focused on the punishment because that is what I dwelled in.

I am now proud to say I really understand my gift of discernment because I believed the voice and tug of the Holy Spirit was me making my own choices and decisions. I thought I had control of my journey. That's how the church made me feel too. I thought because I attended the local church and participated and lead others to participate in the traditions and customs of the church both local and universal I had power to do what I thought was best. I began to study to show my self approved and came to the realization that some of the teachings and trainings and conferences I was a student were in error. This led me to fully seek God for guidance. It was the time I began to spend in prayer and meditation with Him and Him alone that I fully understood who He is and my gift of discernment.

When I accepted my call, I began to work for churches, I had no ideal about building the kingdom of God. Now I know just how powerful God is. He exposed the error of wrong teaching and training to allow me to be able share the true gospel story of His saving grace.

I was taught at a young age about sin and forgiveness, and that is what my focus was when I became a minister of the Gospel. I had an opportunity to serve under three powerful and influential pastors in urban areas; and was excited about teaching and ministering to the sheep who were placed in my Senior Pastor's care. I received several Associates degrees and multiple certifications in Biblical Studies, which made me the perfect candidate for Pastoral Ordination in a local church.

I worked hard in my position as Pastor of Pastoral Care and Evangelism. I developed trainings with manuals, policies and procedures for the Discipleship Department. I noticed that all of my work was new to the church. It called for the church to make changes in their traditions. They were not ready to change the way they did things as it pertained to Christ.

I created unique and millennial friendly ways to show the face of Jesus. My gifts and talents were being used and I was a great asset to my church. I really thought I was doing what God was seeking but I found out that I was doing what my pastor was asking me to do. I became comfortable in my position and started ignoring God's voice.

I was successfully fulfilling the church's goals and achievements but was failing at being a follower of Christ. I knew God was not pleased with me; but I got caught up in the customs of the church and began to become comfortable in just doing enough in my ministry to stay on the pulpit.

I was called on to preach fiery sermons which gave hope to the hopeless and assurance of God's goodness to all who needed to hear that one day all would be well.

After years of doing things the traditional way, God began to challenge me. He first revealed my struggles and then exposed them to the church folk. I became the target of jokes and taunts. All sorts of accusations were on the rise. My recovery journey was tested on so many levels. One of the first things I learned in my treatment program was to remain sober I had to change people, places and things.

I had no idea I would have to consider changing my place of worship. But I had to. The very place I needed to come and worship God and serve his people had become a place that I did not want to be a part of anymore. As open as I was about my struggles, the more closed minded the church became. I questioned my return. The very things I was battling with, were very common amongst church folk. Most thought I was going to stop their parties and reveal their weaknesses. I knew God was making sure I was not comfortable doing the same things I was doing in the church in order to get me to move!

I ignored God for 15 years because I was trained by my parents and all the pastors I served under that I should do things the way they were taught – even if what was taught had nothing to do with what God was calling me to do. After doing it their way for so long I finally had a Holy Ghost Encounter that changed my entire Christian Journey. This encounter consisted of some major revelations about me which also revealed a critical change in my lifestyle and a renewal of my mind. I began to worship God by directly seeking and providing for the needs of His people. My tainted life experiences were exposed so I could reach the lost with no pretense and no judgment. The people who God loves as much as he loves the ones who believe and trust in him.

This out of the box encounter led me to widen my belief system. It opened my spiritual eyes and prompted me to envision a new way of sharing the Gospel. I broke free from the bondage of doing things the way I was taught in error. I began to worship God freely and study His Word like never before. This new way of ministering and seeking the Kingdom allowed me to focus more on God and not on the church which housed the church folk.

The people who are contained in the four walls of the bricks and mortar are the biggest reason I blocked out what God was saying to me because I was taught that my elders, pastors, teachers and leaders knew what God needed me to do so I should follow their lead. But after I had a spiritual and mental breakdown - and like Jacob - battled with the angels to bless me, I let go and let God.

This led me to jump right into my assignment and I felt right at home on the streets of Chicago. Instead of spending time writing policies, programs and procedures, I was participating in movements that focused on sharing the Good News of Jesus and meeting the needs of his people. I did ministry in recovery homes and participated in recovery walks to bring awareness to the importance of seeking help for mental illness.

I talk to people on bus stops, at Planet Fitness and in the grocery stores about Jesus. It was no longer important for me to preach the Gospel in the traditional pulpit in the local church. I had the freedom of talking about Jesus without three points, illustrations and a closing that took the people to the cross, then opened the doors of the church so we could welcome our new members; so that when they would come the next day the doors of the church would be closed (sometimes with padlocks on them.)

There were so many challenges I faced as I began to embrace my new assignment, but I was determined to do what the Lord called and equipped me to do. I began to think of out of the box ways to reach God's people without talking about the church and its people.

I was determined to not let what I had endured while under the guidance and leadership of my religious roots interfere with reaching the lost and - even more - the saved who are also realizing their displacement in the Kingdom.

I live in my freedom of knowing Christ. I am amazed at the amount of people I have witnessed the Good News to since God released me into the highways and byways (the streets) I admit that I was powerless over my addiction. I never gave up on God. I became the person he needed me to be. I took off the pretty dress of my pulpit ministry which kept my calling pure and divine and put on a wardrobe of humility and meekness. I was no longer a title-holding preacher of the Gospel; but a worker in the vineyard.

I remember a young lady I met at a recovery meeting telling me she would have never known I was a minister if I had not told her. I asked her why she felt that way and her response left me speechless. She said, "You are so humble, and you keep things real. You even shared your testimony without shame."

I shared with her that I have not always been this bold. I was taught to hide my truths, my life story and my struggles. But my addictions and my recovery journey taught me how to seek God in every situation I face and trust in His guidance and directions and I can overcome all of them with grace.

I knew then I was finally doing what God wanted me to do. I flashed backed to my ordination ceremony. It was confusing. Everyone kept celebrating the Pastor that ordained me as if he deserved all the praise because he taught me how to become who God predestined me to be. The ordination, looking back, didn't celebrate or acknowledge The God who created and called me.

I am allowed to be a blessing to so many people who may not ever have a desire to step foot in a church setting or those who have experience spiritual abuse from church leadership.

God also let me know I was doing this ministry thing wrong by holding on to that holier than thou attitude I had picked up along the way. He admonished be to bring Deb back, so she could reach His people.

Every struggle I endured I led people to believe it was no struggle at all. I thought if anyone knew I could not handle what I was going through they would consider me a weak preacher having no faith in God. I thought I had to make sure that no one knew I hit rock bottom again and this time I wanted it to end my way (suicide) and very quickly. I thought if I let anyone know I was an alcoholic and God was still using my story to bring Him glory they would treat me like and outcast and ask me to surrender my collar. As a matter of fact, although I never stepped foot in the pulpit intoxicated or even buzzed, I did study His word buzzed or after having a cocktail or two. I never thought anything of it, because I was surrounded by other preachers at the bars I frequented. I've been to Bible Study sessions with preachers where cocktails were served before, during and after.

I believe as a woman of God it is very important to pray earnestly and seek God's guidance to be able to face life's challenges that hinder women to do unpopular out of the traditional boxes of ministry. This type of ministry is certainly a game changer for the kingdom; and a bigger and most critical game changer for a woman's relationship with and love for her Christ.

Debra's Prayer

Oh God my Savior,

I humbly come to You praising Your matchless name. You are my comfort and strength.

I have been through the fire and the storms of life and survived because You were with me every step of the way. Oh, how I love and adore You. I thank you Father for Your grace and Your brand-new mercies given to me each day.

I thank you for forgiving me when I knowingly and unknowingly abused them. No matter the amount of wickedness I faced, no matter the deep sorrow I had to bear, You, oh, God provided me with strength to endure.

Even when sickness and addiction taunted my mind, body and soul, You, oh God, guided me with instructions to recover.

When I ran from Your commands and statutes and did things my way, You, oh God, picked me up even when I hit rock bottom. You put me back on the right track to start over and do things the right way, to bring You glory.

I am forever grateful to be Your servant and to carry the Gospel to the nations the way You created and instructed me to do. With each unique and radical way, I will present Your goodness and mercy to all Your children, the lost and the saved, in a way they will want to know You and grow daily in Your Word.

You are wonderful, awesome and amazing and I will serve You forever.

In Your Son, Jesus Name –

Amen

Undefining The Dress

CHOSEN U. THUMMIMS

"Alleluia! Alleluia! Alleluia! Lord You are fit for our worship, worthy of our praise," I declared. "Praise ye the Lord!" The worship leader led the house in high praise. During all the excitement, I would be called into a deeper level of worship. My spirit gave voice during my praise, "Can I sit you down to dress you up?" Baffled, I could feel my body lose coordination. As I stood still, I heard it repeated, "Can I sit you down to dress you up?" I plopped down in my seat. As burning tears streamed down my cheeks. I was captivated and lost at the meaning of this inquiry. I thought I was dressed appropriately.

About two years prior, I spent time serving faithfully and actively in many capacities within my local assembly. I was Kingdom Education leader, the pastor's favorite choice as prayer leader, as well as the youth pastor and life coach. Plus, I was one of the instructors for the Risen Soldiers (a special program intended for the homeless veterans, addicts, overcoming addicts, and homeless families). With my eyes and heart turned towards helping God's people; I never imagined tragedy would strike. Life as I had known it was about to become my caldron. Everyone and everything I knew and loved became unfamiliar to me. Lives that once rested comfortably in my hands, guidance, and direction, became deprived and lost. What do you do when your call costs you everything?

Only God could help me understand how my closest allies, were the culprits to the destruction of my life's joy - ministry. The daughter I praised, rallied for, and gave every ounce of my spiritual zeal and wisdom was the enemy's greatest pawn. With one selfish decision after another, living life contrary to her spiritual upbringing, she tore the banner of love, trust and faith, I spent years making to shreds. I gathered the family to share the words of the Lord. Looking for a word or proof of consolation that these things would not be. In arrogance and pride, my husband rejected the warning - our union was broken. My children shed tears of fear and confusion at my words. Further drowning in anguish, I listened as the man who vowed to honor me denounced our union, abandoned his family life and spiritual leadership, and openly pursued a double life of spirituality and worldliness. All was lost as I sought ways to hold my head as high as the integrity they were groomed in. It was an epic fail.

What I felt was indescribable. My greatest works undone. Fear gripped me. In horror and awe, I watched my fields ravished without my consent. The agony of defeat was ever upon me. My spirit plummeted to what seemed like the dregs of hell. My faith tested beyond measure. I watched in terror at the depravity of my two most prize possessions - my daughter and my love. I sank deeper and deeper. I looked on until I could find no more comfortable prayers to pray. There was no pretty dress to remotely suit what I was facing. In a moment of despair, I cried out to God, "Father, why has this befallen me?"

In the simplest tone I heard, "You made them your God." My heart tore, I was crushed, lost, broken, and shattered to pieces. Seconds turned into minutes, minutes-hours, hours – days, days - weeks, and weeks – months. The months turned into two years of suffering and trial.

The air was cold and crisp my spirit low as I prepared for service one evening. That night we were graced with the ministry of Bishop George

G. Bloomer, of Bethel Family Worship Center, Durham, NC. My spirit was closed and somewhere unknown. I told God, "Please don't allow anyone to speak a word to me tonight." Hot tears poured from my closed eyes, as I sat in sheer disgust and emotional pain at what my marriage and life had become. When I opened my eyes to my surprise Bishop was standing before me. My heart dropped. He looked me in my eyes, asked my name, and if could he speak to me. "Yes", I replied.

"You're in what is called the second half of your life. God is totally going to redefine, reposition, and reestablish you. But you know about that. There's a huge mandate upon your life. You've had many false starts, then you crash like those energy drinks. You don't know if you want to get up again. God allowed those things to happen to break some things off you. The day you get the courage to tell your story you're going to change thousands of women's lives. You're going to teach them how to make it without leaning and depending on some man." He then asked if I was married and I acknowledged my husband next to me. He then asked if we were pastoring. My husband looked him in the eyes and told him we don't do anything.

Baffled and lost, I sat in the ultimate heat of my spirit. Who had I been laboring with for all those years? Bishop turned from him, looked at me and said, "COVERING IS THE KEY! God says this time it's going to work!"

My life was forever changed in 2010. God spoke, he told me I would go into a season of darkness, my life would be in obscurity and this season would cost me my family. The place I once found solace became my prison. The more I praised and worshipped the more the flame heightened. Service took on a new meaning. For the first time in years, I could not find a meaning for all I had done. How could one known for being instrumental for change in so many lives over the years be sitting in the lion's den?

The best description I can provide is Matthew 10: 34-36, "Think not that I am come to send peace on earth: I came not to send peace, but a sword. For I am come to set a man at variance against his father, and the daughter against her mother, and the daughter in law against her mother in law. And a man's foes shall be they of his own household."

My God, I was standing outside the house I had built (my family structure) praying for eyes to comprehend what I was seeing. My daughter and her father fighting like children. My husband livid and declaring that he was tired of all of us. Every demonic mission came to our home that night and forced me to cry myself to sleep. I prayed, fasted, and made constant supplication for my

> MATTHEW 10: 34-36
>
> Think not that I am come to send peace on earth: I came not to send peace, but a sword.

husband and daughter. It was becoming clear what the invitation to sit me down meant in grave detail. I had no idea how naked my life was about to become. If separation from all the ministerial things was not enough; my teen daughter was now pregnant. I can only describe my love for her as lost; the hatred and betrayal I felt for what her continual actions had taken from me was astounding. I could not stand the sight of her; a girl I could not stop looking at because her beauty was consuming. I lost all compassion. I could not stand the way she smelled, talked, or anything. I felt possessed with the spirit of resentment. It was not the pregnancy that offended me, it was the degradation of her deception that was tearing my marriage, home, and family apart, and had robbed me of my ministry. I had become an ugly beast.

One cold winter morning, I awoke, my spirit as bitter and rigid as the day. I entered the living room there she was attempting to attend school online. I no longer casted eyes on her under any circumstances, she was dead to me. As I passed and came back through, I noticed she was dressed in dark attire. Her head was covered with a large hoodie and she attempted to hold her head as low as she could to hide herself from me. As I approached the kitchen door I was arrested I could go no further. God had poured his compassion all over me. I turned around, told her to stand up and looked her in her eyes. Eyes darkened from crying night after night. I apologized and asked her for forgiveness. I held her as tight as I thought God would. Did things change with her all together? No! The enemy was still at play. The forgiveness was not for her, but for me.

The air was chilled and crisp my spirit low as I prepared for service that evening. I drove my Pastors that night to relieve them of the task, and to free myself from the torments of my closest rivals. The Word of the Lord was swiftly coming to pass in my life.

I sat in confusion. Lord, what story do I have to tell? The second half of my life? Teach women how to make it by themselves? I was terrified. I loved my husband more than life. I could not make sense of the words, 'Covering is the key' (Prophetic utterance spoken by: Bishop George G. Bloomer). How much covering did I need? I was in the house of our covering ministry, I was with my local covering (my pastors), and I was sitting there with my spiritual covering (my husband). On the way, home I pondered what it all meant.

I cried myself to sleep that night but rose with the knowledge of what I needed to do. I refused to present myself any longer before the people operating and transferring the spirits of hurt, rejection, anger, and hatred, you name it, I possessed it. I prayed for a time and was led by the Lord to spiritually resign from all my duties. My pastor and I read the resignation together. He was truly my spiritual father. He looked at me with sad eyes, "I understand daughter, I love you", he said. I thanked him for everything.

Life became still, I had no idea how programmed I was to all the religious activities. The pain, loneliness, and rejection associated with the duty to walk aside depleted me. I was filled with paranoia, anxiety, and unexplainable fear for now being one of those people who neglected church on Sunday. I was officially unrecognizable to those I'd ministered, prayed, counseled, taught, and shared countless hours with. My pastor was faithful in his stead he continued to pastor, visit, and console me. Immediately, I remembered, "Can I sit you down to dress you up?".

As I walked out of fear and into faith, temptations began to come. There were invites to stand and minister before the people of God again in the works I was once known for. Temptation was strong, but my thirst for God was greater.

God works in mysterious ways, He allowed me to cross paths with someone from my intimate past. We had encountered one another a few times over the years, but never lived in the same state. I believe God assigned him in that season to remind me who I was, and what my duty and purpose as a spiritual woman, mother, and wife was to continue to be. Each morning I received a call; every morning, brought a different response. Some days, I was in a pretty dress mood. For the most part, I was pleased to wear the ugliest dress and all its accessories. I was seriously becoming undone. I knew I needed to be saved.

The brother told me he had someone he wanted meet. Sister Fa'reeda, a name I would never forget. I felt contacting her was a big no-no. I feared the rejection I would experience if anyone knew of my dealings with some-one of the Muslim tenets. How could I associate with someone contrary to faith as I knew it? I held the number for a while. One day broken, and filled with despair, I called. We chatted and arranged to meet. All day, I visually prepared for the meeting.

I, being a woman of the cloth should have been well acquainted with the beauty of modesty. However, never being introduced to what modesty truly looked like, I struggled to look as simple as I could. I travelled that night with my daughter and bearer in tow, I wanted her to share this experience because she was broken too.

 When we approached the door, we were greeted with the warmest smile I had encountered in years. "Assalamu Aliakum, sisters", the woman replied.

 "I'm looking for Sister Fa'reeda", I said from behind my companions.

She greeted them and said, "I am she. Chosen? I've been waiting for you."

Fear gripped me. She grabbed me without hesitation, embraced and kissed me on both cheeks and released a blessing upon me. Today, I cannot explain how the love of God held me during that moment. As we entered the room I watched in amazement the love, respect, togetherness, unity, and beauty these women possessed. I observed as the room became filled with women and young girls bewildered how no one wore the pretty dress from a fash-ion, attitude or demeanor respect. Their lives were far beyond what I had been groomed and mentally trained to wear. I was gripped by the beautiful displays of modesty, no one cared what the other had on. No one spoke about their shoes, nails, hair, jewelry, or possessions. There was no com-petition because what I had known in some church settings as the behavior of the pretty dresses was not welcomed. She took me into places I should not have been because I was not of the Ummah (the body of believers). I contemplated why God chose me.

Sister Fa'reeda kept in contact with me. I visited on a few occasions to ensure what I felt was not a result of my emotional pain, over time I backed away. I was not called to minister to them, but to be ministered too. From that experience, something in me came alive, I was determined to understand why and what God had called me aside for. I knew it was not about the naysayers, the fear of others, or all the untruths I had heard previously.

I encountered the presence of God, amid a people the world is taught have a profane knowledge of Him. I knew the gift I was receiving was to strip me of religion and to take me in to my most holy faith. Embarking upon this journey would surely require it. How do I defend what I did not understand? I was blessed to discover how simple meanings can change the interface of our fictitious lives. Islam is a religion of peace. A Muslim is one in full submission to God's will. With this revelation I realized why the presence of God was there, they - just like I - had been called into submission to see if we would demonstrate the power of God through obedience and not our fears.

As I found solace in modesty; I realized I had found my veil (my spiritual hiding place). It was the key to God's Word spoken to me by Bishop Bloomer, "Covering is the key." I had been called to step beyond the pretty dress. It had been the enemy's tool to distract the eyes and minds of those lives I ministered to and touched in time past. It was clear that God was calling me aside to prepare me. The phrase, "Can I sit you down, so I can dress you up" was a higher calling. This second half of life was to be a life of consecration and holiness, a call to lead; not to distract.

First Timothy 2:9-10, admonishes women professing godliness to be adorned in modest apparel. God was redefining all the false comforts introduced and masked as exceptions. He needed me his bold soldier the one who never cared what anyone thought to carry this work. There was a time I did not have the esteem to leave my home without ensuring my outward beauty was displayed. He made me his marksman to show others if I could lay the snare of vanity aside, so could they.

This encounter opened my heart and broadened my understanding from the worldly ideas of what being a Muslim meant. The pretty dress is making me instrumental in the master's hands. I know today, the pretty dress is not indicative of apparel but rather the customs, traditions, stereotypes, and prejudices placed upon females to walk, talk, speak, look, and take on mannerism ingrained to mold and wash us into the perfect imagery of femininity, which have desensitized, and render us captive and open doors to performance, measuring, jealousies, and division amidst the sisterhood that should be established and extend beyond faith, sects, denomination, ethnicity, etc.

My ministry of service to women today is birthed from my encountering the love, acceptance, and unbiased judgment and opinions of the Muslims sisters who demonstrated for me First Corinthians 13:4-8, "Charity suffereth long, and is kind; charity envieth not; charity vaunteth not itself, is not puffed up, Doth not behave itself unseemly, seeketh not her own, is not easily provoked, thinketh no evil; Rejoiceth not in iniquity, but rejoiceth in the truth; Beareth all things, believeth all things, hopeth all things, endureth all things. Charity never faileth: but whether there be prophecies, they shall fail; whether there be tongues, they shall cease; whether there be knowledge, it shall vanish away."

They received me in my most broken and vulnerable time. My work isn't for the healed, but the wounded. My mission is not one of indoctrination but the impartation of the love of God, which should be shed abroad in all our hearts. With the love, kindness, mercy, and grace of God we were drawn.

I am a greater minister for having been broken, torn, and taking into my personal darkness (things I never imagined being faced with), and having God shed light on the dark places of my mind. My experience has enlarged my territory, expanded the borders of my coast. Some may ask, how can I call myself a minister? How can God use me when I've embraced a forbidden belief? My answer, how can I not call myself less than a minister if I received the good at the hand of those who's faith I didn't share, at a time I could not see what was before me? How could I call myself spiritual and not possess the discernment to acknowledge God's sovereign right to place me where he willed, and express his love and kindness to me? It is like the clay telling potter what to fashion on his wheel. How can I walk contrary of the scripture that says, freely receive, freely give? How can I be in the ministry of God and not walk the path of Christ bearing the ministry of reconciliation bestowed upon me.

As women and believers, we need to know the power of our love and the pain inflicted upon those we refuse to share our love with because they do not look like us, behave as we behave, and talk our talk, etc. We are being confronted in the body of faith to change our position and equipped ourselves with the love and humility required to win souls, not to the systems of theology, religion, customs, traditions, denomination, or fear of a title being revoked, but to the kingdom of God. We must empower ourselves with knowing, there's life after being ostracized for going deeper into the call of holiness. There is life even when no one calls us to preach and teach the house down any longer. There is life in being greeted by religious bullies declaring, no denomination; no recognition! In Acts 10, Peter was hungry, went up to the roof top for prayer while waiting to eat, he fell into a trance.

God said, "Rise, Peter, kill, and eat." Peter said, "Not so Lord. I have never eaten anything common or unclean." After several promptings, God admonished Peter, "What I hath cleansed, that call not common." God will have mercy on whom He will have mercy!

The call to go beyond the pretty dress powerfully exposes the barriers placed between those in relationship with the father. It is significant of the veil being torn to allow the woman to beg crumbs from the master's table. It opened the door for the Samaritan woman to drink from the living well. It has empowered me to expand my ministry and reach. I am recognized beyond the confines of the boxed walls; walls that can only withstand what area circumference it was designed to. My God-given reach is beyond recognition, my name is no longer known within the walls, I am known as a sister of the veil (in the secret place and protection of God).

My reach expands each time I encounter a woman or girl who cannot figure out why they are attracted to what they see in me. It expands every time I pass the brethren, secular or of faith and they are forced to look me in my eyes because my beauty is no longer a distraction. I expand beyond the pretty dressed each time I hear, "I love your scarf," and I'm able to say, "It's called a Hijab," "It's a symbol of distinction and modesty." My ministry reach has expanded because like Jesus, he was not afraid to sit with those judged by others because he was born behind the veil, which destroyed the pretty dressed before It could define who I was to become.

I am here to proclaim as the Chosen of God, there is power beyond your wildest imagination if we dare to step beyond the pretty dress. I am the elect of God, 'called for such a time as this'. This is just the beginning I no longer wait for the courage to tell my story declared to touch the lives of thousands of women. This opportunity to scribe testifies, the pen has been lifted and the ink dried. What was written of me before the foundations of the world is being wrought in me.

Challenge yourself to reach outside of your comfort zone, your traditional protocol, and fear (false evidence appearing real) and receive a refreshing level of God, then extend the love of God to those unlike you. As the scriptures states, if you love those who love you what profit is it? My journey is my own, for this work I was chosen. I could have looked at every circumstance orchestrated by God to make me fit for this task and allowed it to destroy my faith. Instead I submitted myself to God and received his supplication for me. In case you are saying, how would I know if God wants to use me? I firmly believe everything we shall become will be manifest and revealed through prayer, that which God desire of our lives will be found and bared witnessed of through his word.

I am blessed today to be used as a bridge to some, a bandage to others, and an introduction to many who just like I before my convergence had no clue how to relate, nevertheless how to show forth the love of God and receive his love and acceptance by women outside of my belief system. What a tremendous privilege it is to teach the scripture to those sitting in the pews having never heard or encountered the power of modesty, its reach, and strength. I am blessed to be walking in my dimension birthed out of my need to be healed. My healing continues, is shared, and multiplied each time I share my story, each time I see those I minister to hearts change and minds open to embrace differences that once explained reveals we are more alike than we have ever imagined.

My spiritual work and goal are to take and expose the pretty dress to as many as shall receive it and wear it in truth. What a reward to understand the workings of diversity, to open the door of reconciliation, to forgive and receive forgiveness for forgetting we are all women, mother's, daughters, wives, sisters etc. that we might minister acceptance based on submitting our wills to be changed, and not our need to change the minds, status, or spiritual orientation of others. The Women Restoring Women Ministry is to reveal to every woman their spiritual and personal responsibility to expose the love of God to as many sister's as possible, that we might increase our awareness and experience the power God has given each of us to advance the kingdom here on earth to prepare us for the hereafter. In the spiritual hope as women we might rear and groom stronger generations of young women who will not have to relive our mistakes but be the forerunners for generations to come.

CHOSEN'S PRAYER

Father God,

Bless us Your daughters for truly we have faced circumstances, crisis, and situations that have us wandering have You left us, can You yet use us, are we worthy of Your presence, nevertheless Your call, will we ever experience life, love, joy, or happiness again.

Matters of this life we're too afraid to confide, or give voice to for fear of abandonment, ridicule, or judgement. Lord God provide us with eyes to see and the mind to comprehend First John 3:2 "Beloved, now are we the sons of God, and it does not yet appear what we shall be: but we know that, when he shall appear, we shall be like him; for we shall see him as he is."

Bless us to remember it's in our suffering with Him that we learn to reign over every situation that has come to disempower us, and at times has left us feeling dismembered in the very core of our beings. Let us hold firm, that "Now" we are the sons of God! We are in a training course. These trials, tribulations, failures, disappointments, and upsets in life, our characters, and minds, have come to make us strong, and to mature us. They are designed to hide us in this making and molding process, to tear us down that He might build us up, to break us that He might make us and not for our destruction.

As the blacksmith beat the iron upon the fiery coals, constructing us that we might be able to say boldly in our season and your timing, no weapon form against us shall be able to prosper, and every tongue that rise up against us in judgement "We" shall condemn, because now we have inherited the right as the overcoming children of God to call down the plots and plans of the wicked one.

That like the scripture declares, in First Peter 1:7 – "That the trial of your faith, being much more precious than of gold that perisheth, though it be tried with fire, might be found unto praise and honour and glory at the appearing of Jesus Christ."

In all things we thank, praise, worship and adore You. We thank you for Your love, restoration, healing, and grace. We thank you for every sister reading this work. We bless You for her deliverance, her testimony, her discovery or her renewal of purpose and determination to fulfill her divine destiny, as she goes forth to share and empower women.

Let us be reminded You knew us before You planted us in this earth, there is no facet of our lives that is hidden from You.

"Now unto him that is able to keep you from falling, and to present you faultless before the presence of his glory with exceeding joy, To the only wise God our Savior, be glory and majesty, dominion and power, both now and ever."

Amen.

Scriptural Interlude

For God is not unrighteous to forget your work and labour of love,
which ye have shewed toward his name, in that ye have ministered to the
saints, and do minister.

HEBREWS 6:10

For we wrestle not against flesh and blood, but against principalities,
against powers, against the rulers of the darkness of this world,
against spiritual wickedness in high places.

EPHESIANS 6:12

And whosoever will be chief among you, let him be your servant:
Even as the Son of man came not to be ministered unto, but to minister,
and to give his life a ransom for many.

MATTHEW 20:27-28

A Letter to My 21-Year-Old Self

By Maria Pinkston

HEBREWS 5:11-14

"Of whom we have many things to say, and hard to be uttered, seeing ye are dull of hearing. For when for the time ye ought to be teachers, ye have need that one teach you again which be the first principles of the oracles of God; and are become such as have need of milk, and not of strong meat. For everyone that useth milk is unskillful in the word of righteousness: for he is a babe. But strong meat belongeth to them that are of full age, even those who by reason of use have their senses exercised to discern both good and evil."

The Night Before My Wedding and Nightmare of a Marriage Began

Dear Me at 21,

I remember that evening so vividly. After all, it was the most important day in our life. If I had the power to go back and do things from a mature Christian frame of reference, our life would have turned out so very different. Don't get me wrong, I am thankful for all the lessons learned, but we made some mistakes and boy did we ever pay so very dearly for them.

You believe that you can have it all, nice cars, fancy clothes, and the happi- ly-ever-after marriage. Those fairytales we read really did a number on us. Such a youthful and naïve approach to life we are living. I so desire for you to just snap out of it. Please pay close attention to the God in you. That voice you hear when you are quiet and still. That voice has a lot to say, but you are so caught up. In love, so you think. You are stuck on the aesthetics, your image, that picture perfect life, filled with all the vanity and fanfare you could ever imagine. Tomorrow you will be making the biggest mistake of your life and you have no clue. You are trying to justify and excuse things that God is telling you not to ignore. Be quiet. Sit still, do you hear him? It is so obvious you are trying to 'keep up with the Joneses' (no pun intended since his last name is Jones). You are glamourizing something that stinks and is rotten from within. You have all the red flags and warning signs right in front of your face, but you choose to ignore them. Instead you are claiming that you are that soul singer Angie Stone kind of sistah, yelling her lyrics, that you holding it down for that what- ever kind of brother. Your bougie college upbringing and rebellious spirit are changing you, but not for the better. Use common sense and reason. Why is it a thrill or a challenge for you to have stuck it out with this 'bad boy', whom you now want to marry – this brotha is an arrested felon, who was locked up and served time in federal prison, in fact he is living in a halfway house and your phone calls are limited to six minutes. If that's not enough he has admitted to you that he threw a television in the window of his "baby mama's" home after an argument. Is this really who you, a college educated woman has chosen as your life long mate? Are you crazy??? Oh, and let's not forget the time you wit- nessed first-hand how he handles arguments with his "baby mama". Girl what were you thinking?

Don't you get it! You don't have to prove anything to anyone. Stop it. Snap out of it. He is no good and you deserve so much better than this. I promise you, if you just set your pride and ego aside, God will provide someone worthy of your love and admiration. So, stop it with this foolishness, trying to be down for the brothers who have been incarcerated by 'the man'. It's one thing to be an encourager and help fight to restore felons' rights, but are you sure you know what you are about to get into? Listen to me, forget 'the man'. Do you even know your purpose in life? How about figuring that out first? God has called you to do and be so much more than the road you are headed down. Yes, God can and will still use you, but girl if you only knew what you are about to face, you would get to running. I need for you to get it together and quickly.

Sadly, that message was never received.

Marriage Counseling Session (after the rehearsal dinner)

It's me again, are you paying attention? Tonight; when Cousin Harry sits you both down for that pre-marital talk, (you know the one that you should have had several months ago, from your own church, right before or at least right after you got engaged) tell the truth, to yourself. Why on earth would you wait to seek pre-marriage counseling until the night before the wedding? Were you too afraid to own up to your own thoughts about your chosen partner? To embarrassed over him being an ex-con? What was it really? The way he dressed or how he pronounced certain words. Hello...my dear self...these were all clues that you were not ready for marriage.

You ignore all these signs and blissfully enter the room hand in hand. As you sit at the round table across from Cousin Harry, who is all set to officiate the ceremony tomorrow, he asks you both what you love about each other and your answer is vague at best. When you see Cousin Harry shake his head, you know right away he thinks this wedding is a bad idea. His face shows one of moral conviction, he looks like he wants to tell you to call the wedding off, but at the same time is afraid of causing a big embarrassment for the family for having to call the wedding off the night before. All this money that was spent, all the family from out of town, all the gifts and money cards stacking up at the house. I can only imagine what is going on in his head if these are the things going across my mind. How could he face my father, worse yet, my mother to tell them both that he feels they should call off the wedding.

I know if they knew back then what I knew about Omar and then heard Cousin Harry's gut feeling they would have gladly pulled the plug on our nuptials.

Your pride is too strong. No way would you consider backing out of something even though you know deep down that he just saw something blatantly wrong with your relationship. Sadly, Cousin Harry also managed to convince himself to go ahead and perform the ceremony.

Self, you try so hard to justify and rationalize your reasons for sticking with this brother from "the other side of the tracks", and I get it, there are plenty of good brothers from all walks of life, but you are trying too hard to be 'down' , 'committed', and 'a ride or die chick', you are overlooking one obvious problem here...he has serious anger issues, and on top of that you know full well he is not trying to be the honest businessman he claims to be. It is all just 'smoke and mirrors'. Just look at how he abandons his own son. You have spent more quality time with that poor child than he on his scheduled visitations days. The signs are all there. Hello...is anybody home...wake up from this fantasy world you are painting in your head. Wake up before it is too late...

Love,

The Free Me

***

ONE YEAR INTO THE MARRIAGE

Well girl, you are one year in and it has been one hell of a ride so far. I see you celebrating your one-year anniversary in Sanibel Island, but I also notice your smile has changed. Is it because your gut keeps telling you that the 'honeymoon is over'. Are you in denial? All the signs are there...he is cheating, and he is no longer interested in being around you. He spends more time "working" at his shop and hanging with the boys. You have enough evidence to prove his interest is no longer with you. You see it clear as day. Trust your gut. What are you going to do? It's just you and his son now all the time. You are a single mom - for all intents and purpose - except that's not even your child. Yet he leaves you to babysit so he can go to the club. Time after time you beg him to take you out, but that always falls on deaf ears. What are you going to do about this mess you helped create? Yes, you made a vow before God. Remember that hesitation in cousin Harold's voice, that one telling you that you all shouldn't get married, well this is that moment he saw but you could not. So, let's discuss this a little further. You all are attending church on Sunday; and yes, Sunday's love making is always on point, but really, who are you fooling? Yourself, for starters. Sunday was the only day he ever took off from work, so all he planned to do was lay around at home. Yes, the chemistry was great, but there is so much more to a marriage beyond the physical. You have been in a sex-ship, not a genuine relationship, it's all that erotic love that has you all caught up in your feelings. This is not the agape love that your heart truly desires. This man is young immature and is clearly living his best life, except you are not a part of it. I mean you keep finding ladies' numbers in his truck, photos in his wallet, and his cell phone records clearly indicate that he is calling this one number and talking all hours of the day for countless hours. The handwriting is on the wall. What are you doing? Trying to be the good Christian wife? Again, let's talk some more. Do your homework, get some good Godly counsel. Who truly joined you too together? Was it God or was it your desire to not be alone, the sex, or the overarching idea in your head that you had to be married like all your friends. You so badly want to stay married like your parents that you are sacrificing the greater part of your life to stay with a man who does not want to be committed to you. All those nights of crying into your pillow, searching chatrooms on AOL and talks those midday with your cousin, do you really want to get help or do you want pity? The tears are more frequent now and every night you are crying yourself to sleep. Things are not getting any better. You are clearly depressed and losing yourself.

***

YEAR TWO

By now you are tired of trying to beg for quality time. It's like he is holding this over you and teasing you with it. Regrets are weighing heavy now. So heavy that you are seeking emotional support from any man or woman who would listen. You and Nate have found your way back to each other. Those late-night conversations are keeping you going. His sweet gentle voice as you reminisce of times gone by are cradled in your memory like a special pouch planted deep within your heart. Oh, how the love you have inside wants to blossom at the thought of having someone like Nate to hold and cherish you the way you can only dream about. But eventually, that feeling gets too hot to contain so you book a flight and fly to Atlanta to be with him for the day. You knew Omar wouldn't miss you. He hardly pays you any attention as it is. So off you go. But a feeling of guilt comes over you. You realize that you are now being just as bad as Omar. Sneaking around for attention from the opposite sex. When your flight lands, you lay aside that fear and as you look into those pretty grey eyes of your true love, all those regrets come rushing back. You pledge your love for Nate once again and swear to him that once you leave Omar that you will be all Nate's. The time comes for the flight back home late that evening and your heart is suddenly back to reality and filled with sadness. As you arrive home, you are surprised to see Omar waiting for you at the door. No sooner than you enter the living room do you feel his hands around your neck, shacking you asking where have you been. Your first thought is "why is this man worried about me now, he never has been before?" Was it because your phone was on silent or had he followed you unbeknownst to you? You were too far gone emotionally to tell him anything that resembled the truth. But would your lies catch up to you or would you get away with it as he did so many occasions.

You have found yourself between a rock and a hard place. This man, whom you love so deeply, has now laid hands on you. He is using chokeholds to control you. But you can't see the forest for the trees because he has you so whipped, both literally and physically. You have turned to your faith to justify why you should stay when instead you need to turn to your faith as a refuge and place of harmony and peace. It is great that you want to honor your vows to God and that is what we are called to do in a Christian marriage. In any other circumstance, honoring your vow would be acceptable. But no, God does not want your life to be threatened. Marriage is not supposed to be one in which a partner lives in a hostile environment under constant threat of death. Stop trying to reason that what you are doing is pleasing to God. That's not right thinking. God wants you to live a life of abundance. He wants you to live out His perfect will for your life. Why do you think he would want you to take abuse? You are not paying for any sins by accepting this treatment. What you are doing is risking a valuable life. Live a life seeking his will and plan for you. You cannot focus on pleasing God when you are worried about when the next incident will take place. The sanctity of marriage is no longer there. The marriage bed and the marriage itself has been defiled. Why are you trying so hard when your very life is no in danger? He is a liar and a cheater. To make it worse he has held you hostage, stopping you from going to work. He dragged you down the staircase. Put you in chokeholds in front of his son. He flung you like a rag doll across the bedroom. He put a knife to your neck and threatened to kill you if you ever left. He left bruises on your face and neck. He has instilled so much fear in you (big sigh). Don't you know that God does not condone violence? You have left this man five times now and each time you went back it has not gotten any better, in fact, it is getting worse. He keeps putting on a show for you. Those flowers being delivered to your job, all those long walks and talks at the beach, the trips out of town, all of these were just ploys used to make you think he was a changed man. But no matter how much you want him to be 'that guy' he simply is not and cannot be that husband you need him to be. It simply is not who he is.

***

YEAR THREE

Great, this should be good; you have finally decided to seek help. You realize you can't make it on your own. The depression and sadness are weighing you down. Crying yourself to sleep, feeling like a zombie never being able to feel the joy behind the fake smiles saying "I will be alright" knowing deep down inside you are losing your will to live. Things have got to change. Perhaps other women from the church can help support you and tell you that you are not crazy. Seeking women who have been married for years gone through tests and trials is a great start to getting the help you need to be set free. You are on the right path. I know this Christian wives' group is where you will find help. Wait what? Did she just tell you to stay with him even after you disclosed that he was physically hurting you? When you told Kathy that Omar was choking you, I am so very sorry her only response to you, was "pray it off." I know it was even more confusing for you when she said her husband spit on her and she is praying for him to change....and then there is this other woman sharing her story of abuse that sounds even worse than yours (drive by shootings, children also being abused, and broken bones) and yet she says she has stayed for 30-plus years. Wow, I guess you are definitely confused now. This group wasn't the best idea after all. No one ever offered any helpful words. Imagine that. A Christian wives' group, that just got together for so-called support. However, but by the grace of God, you are no longer in a suicidal or homicidal. Do you realize how far you have come and who has kept you this long? Yes, it is God. Are you learning to sit still and be quiet to hear from him?

Where can you turn for help? Back to your Aunt's house or to your parents again? Don't feel discouraged about going to family for help. Your mother and father love you and want to protect you. They want to see you happy and not in pain. Your Aunt gave you a key for a reason, don't be afraid to tell her he stole it from you when he learned you were living with her all those times you left. Don't give up and don't give in. You will get the help you are looking for as long as you keep on looking. Please don't be discouraged nor depressed. I know this is hard and it is painful. I know ending it all may seem like the easiest thing to do, but you have so much yet to do and places to see. Don't give up and please do not kill him. I know those thoughts are swirling around your head. But your life will go from bad to worse. So please, keep on fighting for yourself. Help is on the way. Sit still. Don't you hear God's voice. He is telling you this situation is not right. You know you deserve better. Keep waiting, God is trying to help you.

***

GOD HAS SENT YOUR ANGEL

I am so proud of you for continuing to keep the faith. This is what has kept you sane. You are learning to lean on Father God. Going to church as much as you can, will help keep your mind in a safe space (His house is a place of refuge). His word, that you read every night, is your guide and comforter. Don't you feel his presence when you cry out to God from your bed at night. Keep on serving and attending Bible Study. You never know who is watching and how God may send a blessing your way. That series on Moses and him being a Deliverer for his people is just what you need. This will be the moment that tears roll down your face. The first time, you know without a shadow of a doubt that God has finally answered your prayers. Yes, He will deliver you first and then yes, you will be used by God. Start writing down what you are thinking and feeling. Share those one day in a book.

This is your living testimony. Get it all out on paper. God can turn this mess into a blessing for others. Just listen to the pastor, take good notes, buy the tapes, and reflect on what God is saying to you. God can and does use His shepherds to minister to their flock and this is your time for a Rhema word. Yes, this word from your Pastor is a direct message from God. Now is your time to be set free. This is it. The moment you have cried out for many nights has arrived. Don't miss God this time. God has heard you and wants you to know (through the words of your Pastor) that God cares for you and that your safety and peace is first and foremost to him. It's time to come clean. Pastor advised you to tell your parents all that has been going on. All those times you stayed with your Aunt, all the pain and suffering you convinced yourself you had to endure all alone because you were embarrassed that your husband was hurting you. It is nothing to be ashamed about. The marriage is over; and your parents will understand. So, go ahead and don't be ashamed to call them. Share with them all that you have been going through. Your mother has seen your face swollen. Remember? The last time you left him and went home. She knows something has been going on. It's time to own up to all that you kept hidden from them. Let them protect you. Don't be afraid to tell her everything. No, they won't be mad at you for leaving even though the wedding bills haven't been paid off. These were all a part of the faulty thoughts from the enemy that kept you with a man you never should have married in the first place. For now, let's focus on getting you healed and whole. God needs you to focus on Him and being in a relationship with Him. God does not expect you to take abuse from this man. You heard Pastor Tony Evans explain that when a man abuses his wife, he has broken the marriage covenant. Please know that God no longer recognizes your union and you have the biblical grounds for divorce. The Bible clearly tells us that God hates a man who covers himself in violence. Pity him and move on with your life knowing that God cares for you.

Pack your things as fast as you can, call the police to be there with you in case he comes back home. Your safety is paramount. Leaving is the most dangerous time. I am so glad you have finally decided enough is enough. As pastor says, "when you get sick and tired of being sick and tired, you will leave". You finally had enough. You gave it your best shot and you tried your best to honor your vow as a good Christian woman. Don't be mad at yourself for wasting so much time on this guy. Let's focus on dealing with the trauma you went through; these emotional scars will take a while to heal and we need to get your processing underway, so you can be of work for the kingdom. Those night terrors waking you up in the middle of the night and PTSD symptoms giving you heart palpitations as you go to bed each night, well they won't last forever. You will find your way back to yourself and God will lead you down the path of blessings.

When you get older, you will see clearly how this could have been avoided and how you can help provide information to young women in hopes of helping them not make similar life choices. You will teach your daughter and your son how to live holy and not as carnal Christians. You will growth your faith by taking a vow of celibacy. You will learn to listen for God's voice as you focus more time and energy on sitting still and being quiet. He will train you on how to deliver yourself, family, and others on the importance of earnestly seeking repentance and deliverance. Becoming a mature Christian will be your heart's desire and be your passion for living. God will bless you as you bless Him. In the end God will work it out for your good.

EPHESIANS 4:11-15

"And he gave some, apostles; and some, prophets; and some, evangelists; and some, pastors and teachers/ For the perfecting of the saints, for the work of the ministry, for the edifying of the body of Christ: Till we all come in the unity of the faith, and of the knowledge of the Son of God, unto a perfect man, unto the measure of the stature of the fulness of Christ: That we henceforth be no more children, tossed to and fro, and carried about with every wind of doctrine, by the sleight of men, and cunning craftiness, whereby they lie in wait to deceive; But speaking the truth in love, may grow up into him in all things, which is the head, even Christ."

***

I left my abusive marriage in 2000 and that same year God placed it in my heart to launch a not- for-profit corporation, The Soul Sanctuary. We are dedicated to promoting healthy relationships within the faith community. My experience with the Christian wives' group was a wake-up call for me. I knew that God wanted to use me to share my testimony so that other women who may be suffering in silence may get their break-through. I also knew that a big part of my work would need to focus on developing a training program for clergy. They need to be made aware of what women might be thinking as they listen from the pews and how their abusers might justify their treatment while using the word of God to keep them in bondage. When a pastor states from the pulpit that marriage is hard work and you have to fight for your marriage, it may add a layer of confusion for a person experiencing abuse. They want to be in good standing with God but at the same time they are hurting inside and cannot live the abundant life God has called us all to live. Depression may set in and they live in survival mode more than prayer mode.

Since its founding, I have hosted conferences, sat on panel discussions, held countless trainings and lead group counseling sessions for the faith community in Florida and Georgia. Pastors who have never directly worked with a couple who admit there was violence in their marriage may indirectly be contributing to the continued abuse of the victim. It is my hope that any place of worship be open to learning how best to address this issue. Studies show that one in four women have been in an abusive relationship at some point in their lives. The faith community cannot think that it is immune from this societal disease. I am blessed that God chose to be to one of the vessels to help fight against its prominence.

Remember this, God does not desire for you to be in harm's way. Whom the Son sets free, is free indeed. God loves you to life and wants you to have life more abundantly.

MARIA'S PRAYER

Father God,

I thank you for bringing me through all the past heart-aches, hurts, and pains. Your love has taught me to be a better servant, follower and disciple. You have healed my soul and brought me from a mighty long way. I rejoice and say 'Hallelujah' because I have been set free. You delivered me from a toxic marriage and a carnal Christian mindset. I have repented for my worldly ways and You have set me on a new course under your protective covering. I am no longer living out of your will; but have changed into my new 'wineskin' all because of your love for me.

Thank you for your patience, goodness and mercy. I ask, You, to continue being my mind regulator and promise keeper. Use me and strengthen me for my journey. I rejoice that you have developed me to become a deliverer. Allow me to serve as a bridge for other women who may be in unhealthy relationships or still straddling the fence in their walk of faith.

And Lord, for that woman who does feel she is strong enough to leave or is unsure about her future without her abuser, guide her to the still waters and restore her soul. Give her the peace that only you can give to let her know You are with her always. Be that sanctuary for her soul. Help her find deliverance and repentance right.

For the misguided or misdirected living in a state of confusion make clear the path and the direction they should follow and open the door and loose wholeness and a mind of Christ. Let her know that you, God Almighty, are the One who shields, heals, protects and directs, if only she would just sit still and listen for your voice.

What a wonderful Father you are indeed. I give you all the praise and glory and my soul doth magnify you oh Lord.

In the Mighty Name of Jesus, I pray,

Amen.

Moving Through Darkness

CAROL WILLIAMS

I was always the largest child in all my classes. I was a chubby, dark chocolate child. My mother was a fashion designer by no means. Her favorite store to shop in for me was K-mart, while all the other kids were getting clothes from upscale department stores, like Hecht's. My high school years were filled with daily torture. While walking down the hallway a classmate would sound the alarm to start the bullying. "Look here comes Carol." The parade of taunting began again. "It's your world big girl." If that wasn't enough one of the other guys would take things a step further, "It's your class, large a--." "Isn't she a very dark kid." I spent years coming home and throwing myself on the bed crying.

My mother would always tell me I was a gift from the Lord. She had several miscarriages and was told she couldn't have children. She carried me for months before discovering she was pregnant. She said, "In a dream, my mother was walking over this large clear body of water holding a beautiful child and bringing her to me. I knew then there was a possibility of being pregnant. I went to the doctor and was told that I was four months pregnant."

If I was such a gift from God, why did I experience so much darkness at an early age? It started with being molested by several family members. After experiencing molestation, I then had the consistent experience of not only being bullied by my peers but being talked down on from adults.

One day, as I was once again soaking the pillow with my tears, my mother called out my name at the top of her lungs, "Carol, come here I would like to talk you!"

I got up from bed, swung the bedroom door open and responded to her calling my name with such a force. "I am coming."

"I just received a call from the Pastor and he's telling me that you are a fast, young lady. He believes you are going to be pregnant by the time you are fourteen." Her look almost dared me to say something wrong.

"Where did he get this information from? I am not doing anything at all."

"He says he saw you hanging with some fast girls." She moved around the living room as she shared the preacher's warning.

Likely rolling my eyes, I responded, "Momma just because it appears that my friends are fast girls doesn't mean that I am engaging in anything wrong!"

"Well," she continued to ignore my argument. "I am telling you now, that I am not raising no child. If you get pregnant you are going to have to take care of the child."

"Who says I am going to get pregnant?" I am not even having sex?" That truth gave her no comfort.

"Well, I believe the Pastor and he wouldn't make up these words. At the rate you are going to be dead before you are 35 years old." If that wasn't hard enough to hear, her next words dug deep. "You are never going to be anything or amount to anything."

"Are you seriously believing the Pastor over your own child?"

"Yes, I do believe him. I see you as a rebellious child."

She was right, after being molested by family members and dealing with classmates, I did become rebellious and began acting out. I wanted to tell her what was going on in my world; but she was so involved in bringing me up in church that there was rarely time for the real world. A real world that kept me in pain, and it had become time to figure a way out of it.

What was the point of living? It seemed the harder I tried to fit in and be accepted, the further back I was pushed. In the back of my mind, I wondered if I was this miracle child, why was I experiencing so much darkness? I decided that I wanted end my life by overdosing. I went into the bathroom, opened the medicine cabinet and pulled out a bottle of pills. I didn't even look at the name of the pills. I decided that taking the whole bottle would be enough to end my life. Suddenly, her heavy hands pounded on the door! BAM! BAM!

My mother's voice came right behind the pounds, "Carol if you are in there trying to kill yourself, just don't do it in my house." I immediately came out of the bathroom with tears streaming down my face looking at her in a daze of unbelief. I went in my room, slammed the door and cried myself to sleep.

Our friends can't always handle our darkness. I wanted yet again to end my life. I grabbed a bottle of Tylenol. Holding it in my hand, the phone ringing distracted me. After several rings, I finally decided to answer it. It was my best friend Barbara. "Carol," she said it real strange, as though something was giving her information. "What do you have in your hand?"

Crying I told her, "Tylenol, I can't take life anymore and I want out."

Barbara couldn't take hearing those words. She quickly placed her mother on the phone. In a very calm, soothing, but direct tone, Miss Doreen encouraged me, "Life can't be that bad that you want to kill yourself. Do I need to come and get you? I will come now and get you if I'm needed." Her words were divine intervention.

She wanted me to know she would intervene and she repeated the assurance, "Well, if you need me to come and get you I will come and get you."

"No, I am going to try and lay down and get some sleep, so I can make it to church in the morning, "I said this time without tears.

> ## JOSHUA 24:15 KJV
>
> ...as for me and my house, we will serve the Lord.

My mother didn't care how young or old you were, "as for me and my house, we will serve the Lord." (Joshua 24:15 KJV). She didn't care once you got older if it was a different church. You just had to attend somebody's church.

My mother's words would sting in my heart often in my adult age. Heaviness and suicidal thoughts accompanied me for years. Still, I would remember her admonishment – serve the Lord. I would put on the proper church attire and the public face even when my heart felt as if a 500-pound lady was sitting on my chest. For years, every time I went to church, I was upset and angry. I wanted to scream.

One Sunday morning, as I faced my emotional contender again; I honestly didn't feel like doing anything but staying in the bed. Yet, I thought maybe the Lord would send a word to speak to my place of pain. Well, I was so wrong. I can't even remember the title of the message only the words that boomed from the pastor's mouth, "those of you who are thinking about killing yourself, something is wrong with you. I love myself too much to kill myself."

I wanted to flood the church with my tears. I thought, where is your compassion for someone like me who just last night wanted to check out? Who cares if you love yourself? I did not love myself – in that moment. How could I love myself when all that had been presented to me was an ugly portrait painted with disrespectful touches and horrible words? I thought, what does God say about my life?

I sat in my car crying after leaving the sanctuary., "God, I came to the house for a Word from you. I am now pushed back to wondering what the use of living is. Is there really something wrong with me because I don't love myself? Should I just go home and once again attempt to end my life? Lord, honestly, I need direction."

I drove home in tears and laid down, praying that the next day would be a better one. I pondered as I laid there if the pastor thought about the carelessness of his words. Did he even know that his emotions and opinion in that message could have been the last words someone heard before they succeeded at suicide? Did he ask himself, are my words promoting life or death?

The Lord began to reveal that my pain - most certainly - had purpose. In January 2004 I began to use my pain to minister through writing an e-devotional entitled "You Are Somebody Seed of the Month."

I remember hearing the Lord speak the words clearly, "You are somebody."

I said, "Okay, Lord I am somebody."

He spoke the words again, "You are somebody."

That time, I asked, "Lord, what am I supposed to do with these words?"

He responded, "Write a devotional for women entitled, You Are Somebody Seed of The Month. Start a radio broadcast - You are Somebody."

I honestly thought the Lord was joking; but within 30 days, the ministry He was calling out of my darkness was born.

***

From about 1976 through the mid 2000's, my suicidal thoughts were compounded with multiple bouts of grief from a continuing string of deaths. I stopped counting at about 28. One of those deaths, was my best friend Barbara. Oh, the pain of her death. I didn't have a chance to continue the grief process for her, because 13 months later, I walked into a room at an inpatient hospice facility to discover my mother had died.

The first Mother's Day without my mother, I felt like I wanted to preach during a Sunday Morning Service at somebody's church. However, instead of preaching, I decided to write a "Seed," called God is Greater Than the Pain. I sent it out of obedience to Lord. The next day I received an e-mail from one of the recipients.

"Elder Carol, thank you much for the Seed of the Month entitled God is Greater Than the Pain. I received the e-mail the day of my grandmother's funeral. The e-mailed blessed me and I shared it with my mother. She told me to tell you thank you so much! It was a blessing and helped us get through a difficult day."

***

It's important to obey the Lord even when you don't understand the outcome. I appreciate the Lord for allowing me to be a vessel He could use as a writer. I was asked to do a book signing and I remember the Lord giving me specific instructions on which "Seed" to share and to be transparent. I was to share "Think Life." I talked to the Lord about that ministry assignment, "You have to be kidding me - be transparent - right? There are going to be people who know me there. Are you serious?" I spoke a few minutes at the signing regarding what a seed is, and as I was coming to the end I heard the Savior repeat the assignment. I did as He instructed.

Transparency is not about you but what the Lord wants to do in someone else's life. I begin to share my story concerning struggling with thoughts of suicide, when a person directly in front of me begin to yell and cry. I stopped immediately; and two of friends who were with me and I prayed for her. When I opened the floor for questions, what I got instead were comments from those who were attending church on a regular basis and struggling with suicide. I received a message when I got home about how my transparency saved their lives. The Lord is waiting on someone to be transparent, so lives are saved.

It's time to create a safe environment to be honest and be healed. Are individuals around you dying because you quickly want to send them to hell? Is "you are going to hell" the first thing to say when a person confides to you that they are suicidal? Let's stop sending people to hell and calling them demonic when suicide is oppressing them. Let's simply love them so they can live during what already feels like hell. There are dark, dreary and condemning moments, moments of pain, moments of overwhelming and crushing moments of emotion that they need us to pray them through. The smallest life changes to the biggest life changes, can call thoughts of suicide to the surface.

One of those life changes – for me - happened November 17, 2006; the day my mother went home to be with the Lord. I remember everything about this day including the clothes that I was wearing. I was speaking with a girlfriend on the phone and I told her I was going to check on mom, but I would call her back. I walked in the door and looked at my mother laying their peacefully, but her chest was not rising or falling. I realized she dead. I ran to the nurse's station told them she was gone.

The nurse looked puzzled," I don't think that's possible because we just left out of her room." I was right the nurse told me, "I believe what happened is your mother heard your footsteps and the minute you were about to cross the threshold she took her last breath. As much as you wanted to be with her when this happened, it was not her wish." I laid my head on my mother's chest and cried. I have never experienced such pain. It felt like someone snatched my heart out of my chest knowing that I would die.

At the viewing, my mother was dressed in a beautiful white suit with a pink blouse. Her hands were folded with a beautiful, white lace handkerchief extending from her hands. While viewing the body, one of her hands dropped. and I told my family, "I told you my mother wasn't dead."

"Ms. Williams, we apologize for what just happened. We used glue to glue your mother hands and unfortunately it came loose."

"Well, you need to make sure that you fix this because you will scare someone to death." Surely, I was in a bad dream.

The night of the viewing we had worship music playing during the Visitation. One the songs that was played was Draw Me Close to You. For years hearing the song would take me so powerfully back to my mother's death. After quite some time, I had to find another way to deal with hearing it, after all choirs sang it often. Each time I heard the song, I would lift my hands, tears streaming down my face and begin to bow. One of the members figured out what was going happening. He said, "Carol, you either going to go out the door or you are going to go all in with worship when you hear Draw Me Close to You!"

I was home alone one day when I was hit with the realization that my mother was no longer present on earth. I laid down on the bed in a fetal position and begin to cry uncontrollably.

"Lord," I cried out. "Since you will not allow me to take my own life, would you please allow me to die now. I can't take this pain any longer. I am tired."

Assuredly and warmly, my God responded, "I am not going to take the pain away because it has purpose. Try, calling on the name of my son, Jesus to ease the pain."

I immediately began to scream and cry," Jesus!" I am not sure exactly how many times I screamed Jesus. What I did witness is a calming presence enter the room and the pain subsided. The next thing I knew it was morning.

Grief is real and presents so many different emotions. I stayed in denial for months after my mother went home to be with the Lord. I longed for someone to wake me up out of that horrible dream. I wanted to hear that my mother was not dead. I didn't want anyone telling me she was gone on to be with the Lord or that she was in a better place. I wanted her on earth.

Dealing with my many emotions helped me understand - to some degree – the pain of others that I would meet. There were those like Tameika, who was battling so may mixed emotions, after the loss of her mom. She was at the end of her rope. She was angry, depressed, and suicidal. God was using my experience to minister to her sorrow and her darkness. I knew it well enough to assure her that everything she was feeling was okay and normal. I told her so simple but a truth she needed to hear, even if she couldn't take it in right away; that was the Lord was with her and so was I. I prayed with her and told her that she was going to live and not die to declare the works of the Lord in the land of the living.

I made a recommendation that I wished someone had given me, to seek professional counseling. It took her some time, like it does each of those who suffer traumatic loss, but the anger subsided and the ability to function in life without mom began to return.

Mother's Day for years presented a challenge in attending church. It was challenging seeing individuals being with their mothers and being honored. I just was longing to have mother present and be able to honor her. I stopped attending church on Mother's Day for years. Then, one Sunday, although waking up with a heavy heart and tears streaming down my face, I got up and went to church. I had on one of my favorite long length green dresses. The Pastor was preaching a great message that I needed to hear. I went to the altar along with others for prayer. As he was praying, I felt something breaking and I felt the flood of tears washing over me. I felt a scream rising from the pit of my belly about to explode. However, I noticed the Pastor was coming to the end of his prayer and individuals were leaving the altar. I have never been one to draw any kind of attention during church services, so I contained that longed-for release and returned to my seat still feeling heavy. I was going home to end this place of pain.

There is deliverance in prayer. After the benediction occurred that Mother's Day, my friend Toni caught up with me said urgently "Carol, Pastor Tonya sent me to get you before you walk out the door. She said we need to pray for you now. What's wrong?"

I entered a room and Pastor Tonya looked, "Carol, death is all over you and you are not leaving here to kill yourself. " The next thing, I recall is Overseer Lois Anderson laying hands on me and me landing on the floor. She was down on the floor with me, laying hands and still praying. She and Toni stayed in that room praying until I decided to get up. I got up feeling like the chains were broken. I felt liberty! I left having the best Mother's Day that I had in years. Wonder what would happen if we truly prayed for people until they broke through and not be so concerned about our own personal agenda. I believe if we did, we would see real deliverance!

I left feeling great but still felt the heaviness of grief. I no longer wanted to end life and started moving forward. I attended GriefShare which is a 13-week program that deals with grief. I enjoyed the program because I was in a room full of people who all had the same thing in common, - pain related to grief. I learned so much concerning grief and how to include the Lord in every aspect of the process. I didn't know that the group was preparing me to revisit starting a group for grieving individuals.

I began to get calls from friends who referred their friends after a mother's transition from earth. One of those calls led me to Sally. I had lived her story. I could hear even those things she could not put words too. I could almost recite her pain like a script. Holding back tears as best she could, she lamented, "There are days where I feel like I am going crazy and going to lose my mind. I don't feel like going to church or even praying at this moment. I am not sure if any of this is normal."

Another call introduced me to Ethel. Her grief had been holding her hostage and forcing her to look for alternate relief, "I know that I am stuck in my grief. My mother passed 29 years ago, and I can't seem to get unstuck. I am angry; and have had a past of addictive behaviors."

I will tell you the same thing I told both these women. You are not crazy. You are not losing your mind. Grief is normal. Being mad with the person who died and being mad with God is normal. You will feel like He should have done something differently. Prayer and worship will seem impossible to do. You may need to take a leave of absence from church and allow yourself time to fully grieve, and not hide behind the motions and emotions of fellowship. The Lord is your help, comfort and strength, but sometimes in grief you must spend time with Him alone and allow Him to love you back into that assurance.

What you must be careful with is staying in a place of anger. It is important that you find a healthy mechanism to release it. I suggest getting a journal and writing your thoughts, no matter what they are. Secondly, I join the Facebook group Strength for the Grieving by The Grieving. Lastly, consider professional help or a support group like GriefShare.

The timing of the Lord is key. I mentioned revisiting the idea of starting a group for grieving individuals. When my mother transitioned, I felt like I wanted to start a group to help those deal with grief. I never wanted anyone to experience the pain I was feeling alone. I understand that the

Lord is with me. However, I felt alone in my process. My family tried, but everyone had their own obligations; and I was left with just Carol. I was being strong for everyone else while dealing – and not dealing - with my pain alone.

Strength for The Grieving by The Grieving was formed in December 2016. We don't judge. We allow individuals to grieve and move during their process. We keep Jesus as the focus despite how we are feeling. The group has been a blessing to others as well as me. Since the group started, my niece (my heart) suddenly went home to be with the Lord. I am strengthened daily by likeminded individuals to continue moving.

***

The Lord has been faithful to Strength for The Grieving by The Grieving. I appreciate the Lord because He allows me to hear how individual lives are being touched and encouraged to move through the darkest places of grief. Whenever I have moments where I feel depressed or like I don't have strength to make it, I think about the encouraging words of others and begin to encourage myself.

It's imperative that as the Body of Christ we become more compassionate and caring for those individuals dealing with suicide and grief. You may not know what to say or even need to say anything, just be present in a non-judgmental and caring way.

What I learned in dark place is that the Lord is greater than my pain. I may not understand or like the dark place, but my darkness will cause light for someone else.

Perhaps you are struggling with suicide. You are saying, "Carol, I just can't take this anymore and I want out of life. I am not afraid of hell now because I feel like my life is a living hell. I just don't know what to do." I get that. I truly do.

After my mother passed, I went to a Christian Counselor and I tried to say all the right words because I knew that if I said the wrong things, she was obligated to report it, and I could possibly end up at an inpatient psychiatric facility. Thankfully, I did not fool her. I encourage you to get to someone like I did; be transparent even at the risk of embarrassment. Release everything in their capable hands knowing that you are in a fight for your life.

You need someone like that counselor, who looked me straight in the eyes and said, " I know what you are doing. I know that you are having thoughts of suicide and I am afraid at this moment hell won't keep your from killing yourself."

Your counselor can then help you develop a safety plan that fits your situation and your needs.

Listen, beloved, Jesus loves you! I know you may find these words hard to believe but He really does love you. You are accepted in the beloved. You are fearfully and wonderfully made. You are created in His image. You are not a mistake. You are destined for greatness because greatness lives inside of you! I speak to your mind and spirit and command you to live! In the Name of Jesus! Live! You will not pick up the pills, gun or knife! You will live! Live!

I am a living witness that you can live and move through the darkness. You can't do it in your own strength. It's imperative to stop trying to make it on your own; find strength in the circle of a support group, in the chair of a professional therapist, or with a sincere, loving friend. The devil thought the molestation, bullying, and grief would take me out! He tried to use me against myself. However, he didn't win in my life and he's not going win in yours!

CAROL'S PRAYER

Father, I thank you for the opportunity to share my story through writing. I pray for the individual who has been molested and feels like it's their fault. They are feeling guilty and worthless. I pray that you allow them to feel your warm embrace and love. I pray they are reminded they are accepted by you and that you loved them with an everlasting love. I pray that you would begin to turn their ashes into beauty.

I pray for the individual who is having thoughts of suicide. I decree they shall live and not die but declare the works of the Lord in the land of the living. I speak life to them even now. Devil get your hands off their minds. They will have a sound mind. They will have the strength to think on things that are honest, just, pure, lovely, and a good report. Their minds are sound! I speak peace to the confused mind. Peace! Lord, thank you the turbulent waters in their minds is becoming still. You, the Good Shepherd are leading them to still waters. Lord, thank you that their expected end not death but life! Yes, because you live give them the strength to face each second of the day. You promised with long life you would satisfy them. You the life giver be their satisfaction!

I pray for grieving families throughout the nation! I decree and declare that grief will not take them out. I pray you give the strength to grieve and understand it's okay. You understand grief because you are acquainted with grief. Lord, when their hearts are overwhelmed lead them to the Rock that is higher than they are. You Lord be their shield. Lord, be their help. I call on the God of Hope on their behalf. I pray comfort and peace. Lord weeping may endure for a night but thank you that joy is coming in the morning. Lord allow them even in the midst of tears to experience your presence and joy! Lord, in your timing thank you for turning their mourning into dancing. I give you praise that even in grief you still are a grief you are still good. Thank you, Lord, for being greater than their pain!

Lord, thank you for being their God. Thank you for being sovereign. Thank you for reigning in the midst of their pain! All glory to the only wise God, through Jesus Christ, forever.

Amen. It is so!

What Will You Do with Your Pain?

By Kathei McCoy

March 29, 2013 was like any other Friday. I had a standing hair appointment after work right before date night with my husband. That Friday, me and my husband, were going to share our date night with our son, KB. At 7:29pm while under the hair dryer, I received the dreaded phone call that no parent ever wants to receive.

"They shot him!" said the screaming voice on the other end of the phone line. The "him" they were talking about was my son, KB. I was in disbelief, in shock and after making calls to my sister and his biological father, I arrived at the hospital. While sitting in the waiting room I kept telling myself, "Maybe, he only got shot in the leg." "And of course, he's going to survive."

When the doctor finally entered the waiting room after 20 minutes, she said the words I'll never forget, "He lost a lot of blood. We tried everything we could, but unfortunately, he didn't make it."

I slid down the wall and fell to the ground, in a daze. I could hear screaming, chaos and someone beating the wall. It was the sound of one of KB's friends pounding the wall in disbelief and shock. Hoping it was all a nightmare and not real I opened my eyes and saw the hand of the doctor extended toward me. I grabbed it and she walked me to the room where my only child, my 19-year-old son K'Breyan Clark was lying dead of a gunshot wound to his neck.

The next few months would be filled with pain, despair, depression, anger, hopelessness and extreme sadness. While brushing my teeth one morning six months after KB's death, I heard the Holy Spirit whisper these words to me: "Don't die with him." This was a turning point for me. I had to face the truth that my son wasn't away on extended vacation, spending the night at a friend's house or off at basketball camp. I had to come to grips with the fact that I would never see him alive again. No matter how long I waited at the door, he wasn't going to turn that knob and walk in.

Six months after his death, I made the decision not to die with my son, I made a decision to LIVE! It was this decision that restored my hope, got me out of the bed and gave me the resolve to leave my secure 20-year, six-figure management job and start my coaching and speaking business. Because of this resolve I have been on a mission to help women break free from fear, negative mindsets and self-sabotaging behaviors so they can achieve the greatness they desire and deserve. I chose to turn my pain into passion and let my emotions fuel my purpose.

Looking back at the last five years of my son's life, I can't help but to reflect on all the time I wasted being angry, depressed, living beneath my purpose, people pleasing, being fearful and constantly disappointed with myself. I had wasted too much time not enjoying the moments I had with him, pushing him away and wanting him to be somebody he wasn't.

As with any loss, it is natural to experience regret. The feelings of regret overtook me and would constantly consume my daily thoughts. Soon I was weighed down with guilt to the point where I could no longer function. Every time the emotion of regret came up, it won. My mind would almost instantly go to an incident where I wasn't at my best as a parent, and instantly I would feel guilty.

I had so many regrets to come to grips with:

> I regretted not having a lot of pictures of the two of us together,
> I regretted not listening to my husband's advice,
> I regretted the times I yelled for nothing,
> I regretted the times I ignored him,
> I regretted the times I sat him in front of the TV screen and pushed repeat on the VCR to watch kiddie videos, over and over, so that I could have some "me" time,
> I regretted not taking more family vacations,
> I regretted missing any of his basketball games,
> I regretted not saying, "I Love You" the last time I spoke to him,
> I regretted not teaching him more responsibility,
> I regretted not listening to him more and
> I regretted not being the mother he needed me to be.

It became apparent that until I dealt with the feeling of regret they would constantly keep showing up. Each time Regret reared its ugly head, I learned to replace it with a positive memory of my son. I told myself that my son knew he was loved and I expressed my gratitude for the time we had together.

I got my journal and wrote down at least one thought of gratitude towards my son. I said it out loud and I took it in with two deep breaths. I did this simple gratitude exercise every day for the next 30 days. Doing this not only brought back great memories of my son, the exercise gave me over 30 weapons to use to slay the Regret monster. I share this same strategy with my clients to assist them in slaying their Regret monster.

To overcome the constant feelings of guilt and regret, I had to learn to recall and celebrate the good times we had together and all the great things about my son. What I find most interesting is that all of memories I now have of my son are good. My love for him doesn't allow me to experience anything else. These memories are separate from my emotions. I believe this is what the love of God is like – having the ability to separate who a person is from what they've done.

Since his death, I refuse to speak ill of my son or his behaviors. He will not be remembered by what he did but by who he was as a person, how he made me feel, how he lit up a room, how resilient he was and how his smiled made my day. I spend time talking about him with his friends honors his memory. Because he was only nineteen years old, I want to make sure his time on this earth is remembered positively. I don't pretend he was the model citizen, but I don't attach judgment to his behaviors. His short life was full of love, excitement, high energy, traveling, loads of fun, laughter, and family and friends.

Death has so many lessons to teach the living: to live, to love and to celebrate and to honor life. KB lived and loved hard. He was vibrant and full of life. He was the life of the party and boy, could he light up a room. I honor him by not allowing his death to kill me or my purpose. I honor him by resolving, every day to live fully, to enjoy life and to live on purpose.

As much as I have decided to live my life there is still the ever-present internal fight to want to succumb to depression and despair. Even now, I find myself wanting to stay in the bed, cry myself to sleep and give up more often than I want to admit. Accepting the fact that I'll never see my son on this side of heaven is one of the hardest things I've ever had to face. There are days when it feels like a bad dream. The struggle is real.

The struggle to live despite my broken heart, my disappointment and my anger is real. Even on my best day, the struggle is real. The struggle is to get out of the bed, to go to sleep, to eat, to stop eating junk food, to honor my body, to get out and engage with others, to go keep moving forward, to encourage others, to pray, to not succumb to guilt, to not seek revenge, to not be enraged about his unsolved murder, to continue to believe God, and to keep doing my forgiveness work – it is all very REAL.

The struggle is to fight against what is happening in us, and the work required for us to become our highest self. Part of what us keeps struggling internally is the constant question, "Why did this happen to me?" The struggle is accepting that this didn't happen to us but for us.

The struggle is not to stay in hurt and to forgo accepting the greater assignment to allow the loss to uncover my purpose, to develop my character, to expand my thinking and to grow me. It may seem a lot easier to stay broken, angry and wounded, and to wear our pain as a badge or as an excuse to stay stuck, become bitter and to just let life happen around you. There is a constant inclination within to stay the victim and to lose myself in the heart wrenching. My intention, on a daily basis, is to rise, heal and to use my pain as a catalyst for others' great awakening. This great awakening comes when you and I begin to face the pain and start the healing process.

One of the struggles I still have is knowing I have to move forward and the guilt that is associated with moving forward. I feel guilty if I move forward too quickly, thinking that moving forward too quickly means that I'm not honoring my son's death, that somehow, I'm betraying him. In a way, I also have moments of believing that moving forward is a reflection of my lack of love for him. The thought of moving forward can bring up feelings of guilt that you are betraying your son or turning your back on him. The guilt causes me to question whether moving forward will somehow make him mad, will he think I didn't love him, what will others think, what is an appropriate time to move forward and am I benefitting from his death by using it as an opportunity for attention or a spotlight?

As mentioned earlier, the struggle is whether to allow this guilt to bind me or propel me and keep me moving forward. I choose to believe that moving forward honors my son, allows me to heal, and converts my pain into the passion needed to fulfill my life assignment to support other mothers of sons.

One of the easiest things to do is to stay in the pain. It is natural for me to feel the heart wrenching pain, to cry uncontrollably, to complain how unfair it is and to scream at the top of my lungs. I have the best excuses to stay hurt and to stay in pain. No one would dare argue about the amount of pain a mother who had to bury her child she is enduring and her reason for staying right there in the midst of her brokenness. There are those who can't imagine how I'm able to go forward living my life. For others, just the thought of losing their child sends them reeling in heartache. I could easily justify why I don't participate in some activities, go certain places and why I don't attend funerals. I can stay right in this pain and most people would be just fine with that, and times I would be too.

I've watched this play out numerous times - people avoiding me because they don't know what to say. Or you can feel like they are moving on without you, leaving you behind, stuck in your pain. Those that do speak up, with their best intentions, may tell you to move on, that time will heal your wound, tell you how strong you are and how they wouldn't survive if it was their son that was killed. It is rare to find someone who will sit with you and let you cry uncontrollably without uttering a word. So, what I did was avoid conversations about my son after his death. I stopped the tears from flowing when I was around other people and I carried on as if I was ok, even when deep down inside I felt like I was dying.

I now consider pain an invitation for me to fight for my very life. My life didn't end with my son's death and neither did my higher calling and life assignment. When I feel the pain, it serves as a reminder of my decision and declaration to live, of the gift I was blessed with for nineteen years, and the life assignment that is greater than me.

I recall at his funeral, a pastor told me to bury everything with my son that day. I'll never forget that advice and I did just that. After the funeral, I set out on a mission to bury every dead thing in my life and that mission led me to where I am today. This pain has caused me to do an inventory of my life and to let go of what no longer serves me, including beliefs that I am not good enough, not lovable and was a bad parent. In some cases, I've let go of certain friendships and associates that no longer align with who I am now. And I've let go of suppressing my feelings and silencing my desires.

Staying in pain is no longer an option for me. The pain is real, and the pain is there but I have made a conscious choice not to allow the pain to overtake me nor my purpose. If I stay in pain, I will miss the opportunity to help another mother save her son. I will miss the opportunity to enjoy my husband, my family and friends and those connected to me. Now I resolve to:

1. Run to my pain, embrace it, and not run away from it.

2. Allow myself to feel it so that I can heal from it.

3. Use my pain to uncover beliefs and past hurts that need to be addressed.

4. Turn my pain into lessons that support my spiritual growth.

5. Share my lessons to help others heal.

As I sat upright in my bed after leaving the hospital earlier that fateful day, reality began setting in. I asked, "Why did this happen, God!?" This was the question that plagued me. I yelled it, I scream it, I cried it, I wrote it, I thought it and I whispered it! I was so mad at God. I had attended church regularly; served in almost every capacity in my church. I was an ordained minister. It wasn't something that I easily admitted but I was mad at God. I was so faithful so, "Why me God? Why my child?"

I felt like everything I believed was in question. I thought, beyond a shadow of doubt, that my son would live a long life. How could I continue to preach about a loving God that hears and answers our prayers and who protects His children when my belief was wavering? What had I done to deserve this fate? Where did I go wrong? Was I being punished? These questions haunted me and kept me in turmoil.

When I wasn't mad at God, I was mad at those who senselessly took my child's life. Why hadn't they been caught yet? Are the detectives really investigating? How is it that they could get away with such a callous act? This made me even angrier at God. Wasn't it enough that he was murdered? And now it seemed the murderers are getting away with it? Are you serious, God?

It is common to blame God for a child's death. We somehow believe that a loving God wouldn't take our child. The truth is He didn't. God didn't do this to him or to me. I wasn't being punished nor was he. His death was a consequence of someone else exercising their free will, and maybe even of KB exercising his, in the choices he made. God gives to all of us free will. His death was a result of free will. I had to accept this understand that this wasn't about me. My son had his own life and the ability to use the same free will I had and as did his murderer.

Making peace was more about me seeking God with the intent to understand how He could use my pain for a greater purpose than understanding why the murder happened. Making peace required me to surrender the need to stay in my feelings and to understand how to keep living despite the pain. In finding peace with the death of my only child I had to find peace within myself. This meant I choosing to let go of wanting to wear my pain like a badge, using it to get attention, refusing to heal and staying in the bed, in a depression. Peace required me to give up my pre-conceived notions of what my life should look like and to accept that there was something larger occurring if I accepted God's invitation to use my story to help mother heal from their past wounds and to support them as they navigate trying to raise their sons.

Making peace is letting go of the need to be right, justified and validated. Peace is the absence of hostility and an agreement to end inner conflict and struggle. I wanted to end the hostility I had with God and myself, so I had to make peace. Making peace was the result of my decision to release my feelings of hostility towards God, myself, my son and my parents and exchange it for peaceful emotions such as love, worthiness and acceptance, which supported my healing.

A few months after burying my son, I attended a retreat at the home of Dr. Maxine Mimms, my mentor's mentor. She asked me about myself and in response I shared with her that my only son had been murdered. What she then shared with was full of glorious wisdom, "What happened was indeed tragic, but what would be a tragedy is if you did nothing with it." She went on to say, "What are you going to do with your pain?" This question pierced my heart and had me in deep reflection that entire weekend and the weeks that followed. What was I going to do with my pain?

The space I'd been in was wanting to stay mired in the pain, mourning for the rest of my days on the earth. I wanted to blame God and keep my back turned to Him. I wanted to run away and hide under the covers. But this mighty woman's question wouldn't leave me alone. It followed me around until I answered. One day, while lying on the floor of my bedroom, crying uncontrollably, banging my fists on the floor and screaming out in utter despair for what seemed like hours, I decided to give my pain God. In that moment, I gave up trying to figure it out, and trying to determine why and how this could happen to me. And I surrendered my pain using the process below.

I had come to place where I could no longer hold the pain. I gave it to God as an offering. I gave my pain over to God It was all I had, and I thought if anyone knew what to do with it, God did. I opened my mouth and begin to name my pain out loud, my heartbreak, my despair, my emptiness, and my hurt. I closed my eyes, I allowed myself to feel every emotion as I named each one out loud. I made the motions of gathering them all placing them in both hands, I fell to my knees, I lifted my hands full of my pain and with all my being I said, "I give each one to you. I cast them onto you as an offering. I ask you to take them, take them from my heart, my mind and my spirit. I lay them at the feet of the altar, Lord. I replace them with love, peace and wisdom. I have faith that you will turn them into something that I can use." Each time the pain comes creeping back I repeat the same process. I choose to feel whole and I have faith that God will recycle and repurpose my pain.

After I gave my pain to God I started asking a different type of question: "How can You use my pain for good?" "How can I use this pain to bring You glory, and to help others?" Six months later I started a support group for mothers who lost their sons to gun violence, I used my pain and experience to create workshops to help those experiencing painful circumstances titled, "Turning Tragedy into Triumph" and "Surviving the Storm." In helping others, I began to heal. My pain started working for my good and I started to see how my pain could fuel a greater purpose. The very thing that came to break me was making me whole.

The pain also became my greatest teacher, exposing areas in my life that were weak and needed to be rebuilt and reinforced. These areas included exposing true feelings I'd hidden and suppressed, how I had silenced my voice for fear of rejection, and the unresolved and unhealed places within me where I harbored resentment towards my parents that had spilled over in other relationships.

My new commitment required me to get aligned with who I was designed and created to be. This meant I had get free from insecurity, feelings of inadequacy and people pleasing. I could no longer operate the ways I had prior to KB's death: playing small, paralyzed by fear and only going half way. My pain was used to fuel my passion to help women heal and train up their Black boys, to coach women through their pain, and to walk in total freedom in all areas of their lives. My pain gave me the courage to release my attachment to material things, and the old jealousy and competitive inner attitude that had me feel the need to keep up with the Jones'.

Pain can reveal our greater purpose, if we let it. Purpose is using your pain to serve others. Pain helps us connect with others who have or are currently experiencing pain like or similar to ours. It allows us to see others past their outer shell and invites us to meet them at the place of their pain or struggle. Pain can also act like a spiritual laser beam, blasting away the crust and exposing years of accumulated bitterness. We then can transform the pain and make space in our hearts to extend love and compassion to others. Pain can also help you recognize how very connected we each are as human beings, and how knitted together we truly are through our shared human experience. The connection can then serve as a common platform upon which both of us can heal and begin living even more purposefully. Living in our purpose wakes us up in the morning, motivates and pushes us to live through another day, and gives us the strength needed to stay in the fight. This purpose becomes our guiding light and keeps us focused even when pain strikes again. And when we attach those we are called to serve to our purpose, we then have the accountability to keep going when we feel like quitting or giving up.

The purpose revealed for our lives is the very reason we are here in this earth at this present time. If we allow ourselves to stay in the pain, we essentially stay stuck in the past. We will never move forward into the present time which is where our purpose awaits us. Staying in the pain keeps us living in a time that no longer exists, with our eyes focused on our life's rear-view mirror, which is only filled with sad memories, fantasies, regrets, "would haves" and "should haves." The danger of staying here is that you are powerless to change the past, but you are not powerless to learn from it. Your power resides in the present. It isn't time that heals, it is living in the present time that does. Living in the present doesn't ignore the past but instead uses its lessons to inform us, grow us, and make us wiser. We then can gain a better of understanding of the precious, limited time we have been given to walk out our purpose.

I just have the audacity to believe God when He says in Genesis 50:20a, "What was meant for evil He will turn into good" and I was determined to find the Good in this tragic situation. I sought Him until I found Him, and I didn't give up until my purpose was revealed.

I refuse to stay in pain and I refuse to allow the pain to win. What will you do with your pain?

Honestly speaking, the idea of moving forward scared me. How could I live without my son? He was my reason for living; he was my first love. I was sure that he would outlive me. I wasn't prepared to bury my child and to face life without him. But I had to continue to love and live for my husband, my grandson and most importantly, myself. In surrendering my pain to God, I learned that lives were attached to me and that if I chose to die, I would miss an opportunity to help those suffering through what I had for so many years. It was this truth that gave me the courage to face myself and to allow God to transform me so that I could walk out my purpose in this earth.

It was my search for love that brought me to where I am today both spiritually and physically. But in order for me to live again and love again, I fully had to heal, be restored, and also be made whole. One of the first messages I received from God after KB's death was that I needed to be made whole and not just healed. Being healed involved the restoration of my heart from the constant hurting and pain. Being made whole meant that my mind, body and spirit would be in full alignment with who I was created to be. Being whole also meant that I didn't need another's love or acceptance of me in order to have an experience of love. Being whole meant accepting I am loved, lovable and loving myself by having my mind restored to the truth of Who I Am.

I now can love from a place of power and not a place of fear. Loving again wasn't something I thought was possible for myself. My "M. O." was to shut down and stay angry - but God had other plans for me and my life. Loving again meant opening my heart again without fear of rejection or abandonment.

I chose love when the circumstances of my life would have wanted me to hate.
I choose to spend my time celebrating stead of lamenting my son's life, replacing hate with love.

I choose to paint my memories with love and not regret.
I choose to remember his love for me and not the times I felt
abandoned by him.
I CHOOSE LOVE.
I CHOOSE LOVE.

Love is what is sustaining and keeping me. Loving again is a conscious, DAILY, deliberate, intentional decision to re-open my heart, to love fully, to trust others and to receive love.

While standing over my son's casket, all of me wanted to jump in and be buried with my son. It was at that very moment, looking down at his lifeless body, that I decided to live and to not die with him. It was at that moment that the life I knew before his death would be changed forever. Standing at that casket I saw where I had not been fully living but had been merely existing. I saw myself hitting the snooze button, dreading going to a job where I was unfulfilled, I saw relationships that weren't reciprocal and activities I had participated in that didn't bring me joy. I walked away from the casket to become a new person. His death resurrected me.

I decided it was my time to live and to live more fully. For so many years I played it safe. I had a good job, owned a home, attended church regularly and had a husband. I had big dreams of starting my own business, leaving my job and traveling the world but I never had the courage to do anything with those dreams. At that casket, I realized how short life is and how unpredictable it is, and I decided to address every one of the unhealed areas in my life. If I didn't, I would be among the many "walking dead," walking around frustrated, not satisfied with life and pretending to be happy. I didn't want that for myself. I wanted real happiness, not pretend happiness.

The pain of losing a child is a pain I can't describe and wouldn't desire for anyone. The pain is both unbearable and unimaginable. It is my prayer that you first and foremost recognize your son as a gift and your very reward from God. God blessed you with a son. He has equipped you with everything you need to lead, guide and train your son. As a mother you were given the divine role to develop his maturity and emotional resiliency so that he can withstand disappointment, hurt and rejection. The only way you can be successful in doing this is if you are healed and whole. It is literally a life or death matter that you do the "inner work" so that your parenting is not based on your own unhealed wounds and hurts. When you are healed and whole, what you impart to your son bears "good fruit." I know at times it may seem impossible to get his attention and to influence his decisions, but you undeniably have an impact on him, whether it's done knowingly or unknowingly. Never believe that your time with him is in vain. You absolutely matter and are invaluable to him and his life.

I understand that there may or may not be valid reasons for why his father isn't in his life, if that is the case, I urge you to examine yourself. If it's because of you, or if it's because your own emotional wounds or resentment or bitterness towards the father is causing you to interfere with his presence in your son's life, then I urge you to get the help you need to forgive, heal and move on so that your son can have a relationship with his father. When your son doesn't have a relationship with his father, it can turn into anger and rage, that left unattended, can lead to violence, bad behavior, low self-esteem and low self-confidence as he gets older. If his father isn't interested in a relationship with him, I ask you to find positive male role models who can teach, guide and mentor him.

I pray that my story and my pain will spare you the tragedy of losing your son to death, drugs, hopelessness, the streets, jail, a gang, or destruction. I invite you to be the mother and not the friend, to use your struggles to teach him resilience, to teach him to use his creativity and to use his mistakes to teach him discipline and determination. I invite you to not treat him like he is your man but to be the parent. Give him challenges that will spur growth in his character and spirit. He needs you to help teach him responsibility, the value of earning his own money, the consequences of not following your rules, to respect himself and others, to be morally upstanding, to express himself in healthy ways, and how to love unconditionally. Believe me, this will help him become a responsible, fulfilled adult.

Lastly, I want you to savor each moment with him as a gift and be determined not to waste any more time screaming, crying, debating and fighting with him. Instead cherish the time you have with him and recognize your assignment to develop your son into a stable, grounded and successful man.

Because of the work I do with mothers, I have witnessed some amazing changes once mothers have started to acknowledge these dynamics, begin their own healing, and start to engage very differently with their sons. I've witnessed sons return home after being a run-away for months, sons changing their negative behavior at home and school; mothers setting healthy boundaries and no longer allowing their sons to manipulate them into getting their way, mothers accepting their sons for who they are versus trying to turn them into who they need them to be and who they want them to be, and the communication between the two of them being reestablished or improved.

In May 2016, I held my First Annual Save our Sons Summit for Black Mothers Raising Black Sons. The goal of this event is to provide a sacred space to encourage, equip and empower mothers raising black boys. My assignment is to help mothers do their inner work, so they are equipped to love from a healthy place and in turn positively impact the emotional well-being of their sons.

KATHEI'S PRAYER

Dear God,

First and foremost, I want to thank you for who You are. I thank you for allowing us to become mothers of sons, what an awesome burden and responsibility. I will be honest and say at times we do not feel equipped in ourselves, we are not, but with You all things are possible. Holy Spirit help us to surrender our will to Yours for our sons. Give us the tools to train him up in the way that he should go. Help us to heal ourselves from any and all past hurts, confusion, misunderstandings, unforgiveness, bitterness or anything that is not like You, so we do not knowingly or unknowingly influence our sons negatively. Allow our sons to see us becoming healed so they know that, with You, they can be healed too.

God, I thank you for our sons' fathers. I thank you that You saw fit for us to bring these beautiful children into the world. I ask that You strengthen and heal our relationships so that our sons can see how two adults are able to share in the responsibility of raising a son. A mother cannot and should not do it alone. Nor should a father feel as if he has no one to support him. If there is anything that we have done to hinder the relationship between our sons and their fathers, please forgive us and help us to remedy that situation. You implore us in the word to do all that is in our power to live in peace with everyone. Holy Spirit please help us to live in peace with our sons' fathers.

God, we need Your help becoming the best parents we can be. The world says that we should be their friend, but we know what our sons need are parents. Help us to give them what they need and not always what they want. Help us to create safe, and clear boundaries. Help us to be consistent in the standards that have been set. Help us to reach out to people and not be ashamed of what might be happening. Please put people in our path who can support us and teach us to be the best parents we can be, then Lord help us to accept the information given to us with the understanding that they only want the best for us and our sons.

God help us to cherish every moment You have given us with our sons, help us to focus on the positive things they are doing, and the areas of growth as opposed to always pointing out what is wrong. Help our relationship to grow stronger. We know that we cannot do this alone and that we need the help of the Holy Spirit; so please Lord have Your way.

God remind our sons who they are, strong and courageous warriors, who can accomplish anything; bright and mighty, fearfully and wonderfully made to be everything You created them to be. Help us to recognize and stir up their gifts and to nurture their strengths so they can walk fully in their divine purpose.

Amen

Obeying the Great Commission – Missionary Arriving for Duty

JANICE LEWIS

MATTHEW 28:18-20: *"Then Jesus came to them and said, "All authority in heaven and on earth has been given to me. Therefore, go and make disciples of all nations, baptizing them in the name of the Father and of the Son and of the Holy Spirit, and teaching them to obey everything I have commanded you. And surely, I am with you always, to the very end of the age."*

***

Charles Spurgeon, a Baptist preacher from the 1800's once said, "Without God we should fear to move; but when He bids us go, it would be dangerous to tarry." This is where the turn in my life June 2003 originated from. I had been saved for over 16 years before I SERIOUSLY began my walk with the Lord. For many years I had heard the call of God telling me that the work

I was doing was completed and that He had already made another level for me. He also told me that I had to prepare to walk into that new level. I, however, was quite complacent with a great job, nice home, and most of what the Jones' had.

Back in 2003 when all "hell" literally was breaking loose in my career and family, I decided to seek God's face for the call upon my life. I laid flat on my face and I remember thinking as I was going down, "I wonder if this carpet is dirty and should get a towel to cover it." Well I didn't get a towel and felt that it was about time for me to get dirty if that what it took. I lay there - listening. Too many times I had gone on my face before God telling or asking Him for something I either wanted or needed. This time I listened! The Holy Spirit spoke to me and told me what I needed to walk in the calling I was placed on this earth to do. From the time I raised myself off of the floor, I have not looked back. The journey hasn't been all good, but I would take nothing for it and I mean nothing.

I was born in a three-bedroom home in Magnolia, MS to parents, Joe and Ruth Robertson, who were devout Christians. My Mamma received a Doctorate in Theology on her 79th birthday in 2005. I have 11 siblings. Mama and Daddy raised us in the church. We went to Church, Sunday School, Prayer meeting, Bible Study and all of us sing in the choir. They didn't give us a choice.

At 17 and after graduating from high school I decided to get married. I had a bit of a rebellious spirit. (I haven't always been SAVED.) After high school, I attended Grambling State University/Louisiana and onto the University of Southern Mississippi where I graduated with a degree in Journalism/Advertising. The day after graduation I took a job in Yosemite National Park selling advertising inside the park and other odd jobs. I always loved the Word of God even though I wasn't saved, I loved reading the Bible and often wondered what this "becoming a Christian and being saved."

After moving to Washington, DC from California, I was so awesomely blessed to get a dream job at The Washington Post. I interviewed on a Wednesday and was hired on the following Monday, eventually becoming a Bureau Manager. I wrote a weekly people's column and overall loved the job. If I had really been paying attention way back then I would have realized that God was treating me very special. God blessed this country girl from Mississippi to work with one of the top five newspapers in the world.

Well, as life ran its course, September 4, 1983, God gave me a gift of – A BABY BOY. Having been a fan of the TV show Dynasty, I named him Kerrington. Life had its ups and down and through the downs I started to read the Bible more and more. I found solace in the Word of God. Finally, in the midst of going through a divorce, I knew that only God could heal the wounds. On December 26, 1987, I gave my life to the Lord. I told God I would serve Him if He would only relieve the pains of life at that time. He gave me peace and I started to become much more serious about life.

Moving to Florida with a young son, I had to grow up real fast and soon realized that I needed to be like my Mama, who didn't have all the answers but always sought the Lord for guidance. I started to read the Bible more and more. Randomly one-day God guided me to Barry University. I conversed with Theology Department Priest, Father Ed, telling him that I wanted to know more about the Lord, so I could work at being a better Christian. I wanted to be governed by the Holy Spirit in all that I was doing. I graduated with a Master's degree in Theology and for the first time in my life I started to have more discernment of scripture and what the Holy Spirit was all about. I wanted more to please the Lord in everything that I did. I understood what it meant to give God the glory in all I do. But, it didn't happen all at once; but praise God – it happened.

Part of it happening came in 1988 while attending a revival at the New Birth Baptist Church in Miami, Florida. On that particular night, Rev. Jackie McCullough was the evangelist. As I stood with my hands raised and calling on the name of Jesus something strange happened. As I was trying to praise Jesus - the Holy Spirit had gifted me with speaking in tongues! Every time I tried to speak in a normal sound, it came out in a language that was not native to me. I felt overwhelmed. My body felt warm and I felt like breaking loose and running around the church which many people were doing.

As soon as church was over, I rushed to my car. I got into the car and tried to pray my normal way. It didn't happen. I was really loud and continued to pray in the Spirit. I called my friend who is a minister and she told me not to be alarmed but to trust that God was taking me to a new level in how I am to SERVE HIM. I prayed all the way home in the Spirit and into the night until I fell asleep.

So, the night I laid prostate listening and not asking for anything I had fallen asleep and awaken. When I got up off of the floor, something was different. I remembered what I had heard while praying and seeking God. The Holy Spirit instructed me to sell my condo. I knew totally that I wanted to serve God in whatever capacity He wanted me to. The next day I found myself walking around the condo praying in the Spirit as the constant thought lingered in my mind of selling the condo. I thought to myself, where is this coming from? I was at a desperate place in my life where I needed CHANGE! As I went to bed that night I found myself telling the Holy Spirit, "If you give me a sign about selling my condo, I'll go and serve you in Africa." You see, I had long wanted to return to Africa on a mission trip, after my first encounter there. Never did I imagine I would be doing it full-time.

Not only did I ask Him to sell the condo, but I added eighteen thousand dollars more than what the last unit in our area sold for.

Three days after putting the condo on the market, it sold. The man was offering CASH. I was shocked. Not only did it sell, but the buyer asked if he could keep everything in the unit, except my personal stuff. He was going to give it all to his daughter as a wedding present. The buyer wanted to close in three weeks, so his daughter could move in right after the wedding. I didn't know what to do. After receiving the offer, I sat down the next night to pray and realized that God indeed had His hand in this. I called my Mamma and told her what had happened. She told me, "You have to be careful what you ask the Lord for."

God did it so that I would move immediately toward Serving Him. Because I wasn't expecting to sell my condo, and especially not so quickly, for almost eight months, I ended up having to live from one friend's home to another. I began to research Foreign Missions through National and American Baptist. I knew the Holy Spirit was telling me to serve in Africa.

The summer of 2003 I met with the late Dr. Mack King Carter, who was the Senior Pastor of the New Mt. Olive Baptist Church, in Ft. Lauderdale, FL. I told him I had been called by God to be a Missionary. I started to cry as

I told Dr. Carter that I was being led by the Holy Spirit to go and serve in the foreign missions' field. I didn't have any fear of it, but many preachers, friends and acquaintances warned me, "Africa is dangerous." "There are so many AIDS cases." "That's too far for a woman to be alone..."

Dr. Carter was silent, and I could see him wiping his eyes. His voice quivered a bit and that's when he said, "I know this is nobody but God because I've been told on numerous occasions to place a missionary, full-time on the Foreign Mission Field." He said he had prayed about it and felt that He would leave this earth, being disobedient to God. The tears were welled up in Dr. Carter's eyes. We both cried. Dr. Carter then told me He would get on the phone immediately with the National Baptist Association to see if I could fly to Philadelphia for an interview to see if they could place me right away.

It took about two months for the interview, but I was hired right away. Still weeks went by and

I didn't hear anything. Dr. Carter and I called constantly checking to see if any particular area was available. As I waited, National Baptist gave me names of people that had served on the Foreign Missions field and the few that were still there. I contacted all of them and told them the plight of how the Holy Spirit was leading me.

I was introduced to a lady, Debra Towne, who later became my mentor. She was serving as a full time missionary in the Congo. She and I exchanged emails daily. I asked tons of questions and she gave me advice. She was very direct and told me this has to be a calling, because otherwise I would end up back in the U.S. I knew without a shadow of a doubt; the Lord was giving me His Divine Guidance and Direction. I felt it in my soul.

Five months went by and I sat down with Dr. Carter and informed him that the Holy Spirit was guiding me to go on my own to Nairobi, Kenya. Dr. Carter was a little uncomfortable with that. I told him, the Lord will be with me and told him the Holy Spirit has told me to go NOW and don't delay. One night while praying, I set my focus on: James 1:27 "Pure religion and undefiled before God and the Father is this, to visit the fatherless and widows in their affliction, and to keep himself unspotted from the world."

Dr. Carter told me if that is what the Holy Spirit had given me that is what it would be. He said he definitely would not try to change my mind. One month after that meeting, June 6, 2006, I boarded a plane, alone, to Nairobi, Kenya. I knew only one person and that was a safari driver. His name is James and when I had visited Kenya years before, he had driven us in a taxi around town. James would send an email over the years to say hello. We kept in touch.

I literally went, being led by the Holy Spirit, knowing the Lord had opened the doors that needed to be opened in Kenya, and slammed shut the ones that needed to be closed at home. Three months before I left the US, a preacher friend of mine told me about a couple in Kenya. The man was a preacher and his wife worked with him. She gave me their email and we started to communicate. I had expressed to them that God was leading me to work with orphans and widows. The preacher shouted out loud! That is the focus of his ministry. I informed him that I would like to look at their project and maybe we could do some sort of partnership.

I informed a friend I met after considering a position with Wycliffe Bible Translators, that I was going to Kenya but didn't have any place to stay. She shared that Wycliffe had a large campus and would often rent rooms to people. I stayed at the Wycliffe Campus for the first two weeks. Then I was blessed to stay a couple of weeks at the Desmond Tutu House in Nairobi. After the fourth week, I found an apartment very close to the church I later joined, near friends I met and the major throughway that allowed me to travel to the villages.

I informed James, my driver and friend, that the Holy Spirit was leading me to go to where no one else had gone. Go reach the unreached; go to the areas where they had not heard the gospel and to where they needed the most help. The Preacher, his wife and I finally worked together and started a feeding program with what was supposed to provide for 150 orphans but ended up serving 250. I started the feeding on Saturdays only. I purchased food and we rented a warehouse. The food was from floor to ceiling. Every Saturday, about 90 Widows came around six in the morning to cook beans and rice. We made everyone tea (which is their staple). We did that for about 15 months. One week the widows informed me that they did not have enough food left to cook for even 100 children. I was shocked.

During the same time, the driver informed me that I was being taken advantage of because the majority of the children there had both parents. He snooped around and found out that the Pastor didn't have a ministry but had formed one when he knew I was coming to town. A month before I was arriving, he went door to door and told the people he wanted their children to pose as orphans and told the married women they had to act as widows. Every week the children would spend about six hours with me. I purchased soccer balls, games and all types of recreational and educational items. I taught them songs from our church and we held worship service every Saturday before eating. I would preach some Saturdays and the preacher the others.

Members of New Mt. Olive Baptist Church bought brand new sewing machines for me. The widows used them to make outfits that I would bring back and sell to the church members, along with jewelry. We put lots of money back into the project. Sadly, I discovered that the preacher partnering with us had been taking some of the food and selling it to pay for his two children's school fees. He had also been taking food home to eat. Of course, I was devastated. I asked the preacher about the incident and he broke down and cried along with his wife. This was my first introduction to foreign missions. I am so glad God allowed everything to happen just the way He did. After that incident, everything I did had to be prayed about for months. Some projects took years to begin, because it took years before trust was restored.

We now serve in 13 different villages impacting about 13-thousand lives through the non-profit organization Project Hope Global Outreach. I have 18 Kenyan staffers, one full-time Kenyan who oversees all of the projects, and one American who pays the bills. Yet, I thank God that we were there to help lead over 35 former witches to Christ and witness them be born again.

I am so grateful for the calling on my life and wouldn't trade it for nothing in the world. Yet, there was another battle I would have to fight. In 2013, I was diagnosed with stage four blood and bone cancer, I had to have close to five years of chemotherapy and an extended period of radiation. In 2016, I was blessed to be admitted to the Mayo to have my stem cells harvested. Six days later, I went into and remain in remission.

I returned to my widows, children and staff to continue being used by God in such an amazing way. I am continually humbled because He called and chose me as His servant. The best feeling in the world is to know what you were birthed for a powerful purpose. I will serve Him until I either get up out of a grave or am caught up in the rapture.

Project Hope Global Outreach Inc. is thriving. We have built a brand-new library / welcome center and teacher's lounge at our school in Bissil. It is in the Masai community. It will accommodate over five thousand people in the community.

We also now have a volunteer nurse that provides services like free physical examinations, HIV/AIDS testing and counseling, and prevention intervention.

I welcome each and every one of you to fellowship with me in Kenya on the missions' field. I promise when you come, you will not be the same upon your return, if you return. Proverbs 16:3 – Commit to the Lord whatever you do, and your plans will succeed. I have a strong desire to serve in Africa for the rest of my life and I am here for God's people as long as He allows.

JANICE'S PRAYER

Dear Lord,

I thank you for the calling You have placed on my life. Thank you for choosing me. I am truly humbled. I ask for Your Divine guidance and direction, as I am obedient in serving Your way, Your will and in Your time. I want to be pleasing as in every way to serve You as you have commanded in the Great Commission.

Lord please open the doors to those who believe they are called to do missions nationally and internationally. Father, the labor is plenteous, and more laborers are needed. Jehovah Jireh, please grant funding for passports, Visas, travel shots, airline tickets and fees, and for everything that will be needed for Your work in the field. Lord please send sponsors that will assist me, and other missionaries around the globe financially. Send prayer warriors to keep us lifted to you. Please provide other believers so that we can share the Good News of Christ even more.

Lord, there are so many like me, who long to do more for Your Kingdom, more for those who may not have comfortable places to worship or live; those in depressed and war-weary areas. Help us Lord God to fulfill the plans and the purpose You have set us apart for. Please Holy Spirit lead and guide us in every way as we serve those who are less fortunate. Let us sincerely give them Your plan of salvation and the gospel, as You have instructed in the Word of God.

Romans 10:9

That if thou shalt confess with thy mouth the Lord Jesus, and shalt believe in thine heart that God hath raised him from the dead, thou shalt be saved.

Holy Spirit send me, my fellow missionaries, and those called and preparing to enter this work to the Jerusalem, Judea and Samaria areas - lead us to the places where those that have not heard Your Word live; and to those areas that need assistance in understanding it. Holy Spirit, You have said we must touch the ends of the earth before Your return. Help Your evangelists and missionaries, and those being raised up enough to enter the missions' field to stay willing, ready, and obedient to where You lead us. Help us to remember this work is not about financial profit; but about souls won for The Kingdom. Dear Lord, keep our motives and intentions pure.

Holy Spirit let us be patient and respectful as we learn different cultures and languages. Teach us how to pray against all satanic forces, evil spirits and witchcraft. Let the people hunger for Your Word. Please remove all obstacles that may try to hinder Your Word going forth. I pray Psalm 91 for total safety and to stop all opposition that may try and cause harm to every missionary on assignment. Change every heart that may have hatred or seek violence towards me and all missionaries.

Let Your Word spread rapidly. We know it will not return void. Father, let there be even one who yields to You, becoming transformed so heaven can celebrate.

Holy Spirit help me and Your purveyors of The Word to teach and do missions not only nationally and internationally, but to our next-door neighbor.

Thank you, God for choosing me and for the calling You have placed on the lives of others to heed the charge to go ye therefore and share the gospel as a missionary. Let Your work be accomplished through Your grace and mercy. May lives be transformed through Your servants as we extend salvation, grace, mercy, compassion and new life.

In the name of Jesus, The Christ, I pray;

Amen

Scriptural Interlude

For, brethren, ye have been called unto liberty; only use not liberty for
an occasion to the flesh, but by love serve one another.

GALATIANS 5:13

Unto whom it was revealed, that not unto themselves, but unto us they
did minister the things, which are now reported unto you by them that
have preached the gospel unto you with the Holy Ghost sent down from
heaven; which things the angels desire to look into.

FIRST PETER 1:12

Let love be without dissimulation. Abhor that which is evil; cleave to
that which is good. Be kindly affectioned one to another with brotherly
love; in honour preferring one another; Not slothful in business; fervent
in spirit; serving the Lord; Rejoicing in hope; patient in tribulation;
continuing instant in prayer; Distributing to the necessity of saints; given
to hospitality.

ROMANS 12:9-13

Process of the Seed - Take Root

KIMBERLY MCGREW

My family and I would always spend summer vacations in Tyler, Texas, at my grandparents' house. We would arrive to their home with great expectations for the summer. Immediately, we would find ourselves in the backyard where grandma would be picking from her garden. She would pick all sorts of vegetables for dinner. I was always amazed at her garden and how patient she was in maintaining it. Also, in the backyard was the biggest apple tree! Though we had great expectations for the summer, my grandfather believed teenagers should be working in the garden the entire summer. You see it's easy to watch someone garden until you have tried it for yourself. The planting process is a learning skill that you have to acquire a taste for.

My mother would say, "Kim, just be still and watch. You will learn more than what you bargain for." I am eternally grateful of the lessons learned about sowing seeds and being patient wait for the harvest. As I reminisce I remember that every plant had its own time and season to grow. In Eccle-siastes states to every season there is a time for something.

I would always hear how the time and season was significant, but I never heard of the root system of the plant or tree. And, how the root must go deep in order to maintain its sustainability. In my research I learned a tree's root system can extend a long way from the trunk, far beyond the edge of the crown. Therefore, a tree can have hundreds of miles of roots, some as thin as a human hair; however, it's the expansive territory of the root that excites me.

Each tree in our grandparents' garden bared fruit. However, the apple tree had taken over the backyard so that we could pick apples without climbing the tree. They would call this low hanging fruit. This tree had taken over so much territory it invaded their neighbor's backyard. The other thing that excited me about this root study is that in order for trees to withstand storms, the root had to dig deeper; further when planting seeds, the deeper the seed is planted the less likely a storm will disengage it. Once the seed is planted, it doesn't think twice about why it was created. It goes underground and takes over the territory that it is given in order to bear fruit for others to enjoy.

I also remember climbing through the tunnels, playing hide-n-seek with my cousins. We would also spend time looking for the spotted touch-me-not flowers that were along the shaded areas of the neighborhoods. These flowers were amazing to watch. Part of their growth process was to shoot forth seeds. If you touched these flowers before maturity they would die. However, if the flower was touched during the mature stage it would build off of the touch and grow stronger.

God gives me insight – even now – on how the success of the gardens that my mother and grandmother tended was clearly because they understood the power of the seed.

We as the daughters of God are the seeds that He has shot forth in the earth to take over the territory that He has planted. God as The Master Gardener knows the power in each of our seeds. He knows our potential, skills, quirks, and even our hang ups. He knows what lies on the inside us and understands who we are and who we are meant to be.

146

We are God's garden and he has planted seeds that will sprout in His season. We must have patience and trust that He will bring forth the fruit in its season. The seed you carry is where God has locked your true identity. That seed is your divine connection, and the assurance that like the Bible says there is nothing, neither death nor life that can separate you from the love of God.

The enemy will plant his seeds of discord around you to distract you and give you a false identity and steal your purpose. Still, stay rooted and thrive where you are planted until God moves you to new ground. Be reminded that anytime during transition your identity will never be mistaken.

Germination is the **process of seeds** developing into new plants. First, environmental conditions – like shaded areas - trigger the **seed** to grow. As a youth pastor I had a part-time job working in a detention center. I would pray daily on how I could be a beacon of light to those whom I would engage. The Detention Center was clearly a shaded area. Shaded areas are places that limit our God-given ability to grow and be successful.

As I walked into the center, with an eager eye, I would search out who I could recruit for the night to plant seeds of wisdom. We were sitting in a meeting when I noticed a youth that was distant. As I engaged him in conversation I asked why he was incarcerated. I felt in my spirit that he was placed they're through ill matters. He explained to me, that his father had picked a fight on purpose so that he would get picked up. I was puzzled about why his father would do such a thing.

The teen explained that he had given his life to Christ and had refused to smoke weed with his father. He had begun praying that God would intervene. I felt my spirit leap in agreement. God began to deal with me in that moment. I told him, "I think I am here for you, because I was called in to work on my night off."

As I begin to minister to him, God began to work in the parole officer's department. As it turns out, that night we had to lock everyone down. Yet, God gave me a vision that the doors of the jail would open, and the teen would be released. God will send us into places unknown or undesired with a word to set the captives free. As I opened the doors of his room after the lockdown, I felt the power of God. I explained to him how proud God was of him for taking a stand before his earthly father so that his Heavenly Father will be glorified. Ministering to him in that facility was a test for me. It was not something we were supposed to do in the workplace. When God speaks, we as the seed of God must respond. I pointed my hand toward the teen and prayed the power of release and deliverance over him. He fell to the floor weeping and thanking God for His power. The next morning, he was released.

The power of God is sharper than any two-edge sword. In order for the seed to grow the ground may be triggered for growth. To be triggered the ground has to tilled, disrupted, cultivated, worked, farmed, plowed, dug, turned over and prepared. All of this happens so that we fully embrace and know thyself! If you don't know who you are you will easily convert into whatever life hands to you.

As I have journeyed through life I was faced with health and life scares that made me second guess who God was, and did He actually exist. Life traumas that were unimaginable for any believer to experience. Sickness struck my body and mind where doctors thought my diagnosis was irreversible. While sitting on a hospital bed, doctors delivered some devastating news. They said my memory would dissipate and I would not remember nor be the vibrant woman I once was. As my memory and health were deteriorating, I could still hear my spirit praying against the words the doctors proclaimed over my life. You see, regardless of how life may strike the seed, the Holy Ghost who holds my true identity, still lives on the inside of me. The Master Gardener could speak to the internal physiological trauma and remind it that I am not born of a corruptible seed. Until, I could command it myself, The One who planted the seed, still declared I was living and abiding in the word of truth; and I would operate in regeneration and sanctification.

For you have been born again, but not to a life that will quickly end. Your new life will last forever because it comes from the eternal, living word of God. Be mindful that all things happen for a reason and it gives you validity that God trusted you to survive the process and be the voice that will deliver others out of a similar situation. You were planted – you were not buried. If I had never been sick, I would not know God as a healer. If I never

148

knew hardship in my life I would not know God as a way maker. We are seeds of the God and when He gave us dominion over the earth, He gave us authority to take over territory – like expansive and long-settled roots - even when the enemy strikes.

> **HEBREWS 12:1**
>
> Wherefore seeing we also are compassed about with so great a cloud of witnesses, let us lay aside every weight, and the sin which doth so easily beset us, and let us run with patience the race that is set before us.

There is nothing more unsettling than trying to become something that you were not born to become. That's called mistaken identity. A rose is not planted to be like the tulip. It was planted and grew from a seed that held its required makeup. It became what it was planted to be. Overcoming people's voices and their opinions of who they think you should become is false identity. There were times when I couldn't hear Gods voice because it was crowded out by those who I kept company with. This brought an unsettling in my spirit where I had to get away and heal properly.

How many times do we go to God complaining about labels that came from passing seeds or dead roots that we encounter? These false accusations and invitations to a false or mistaken identity leave us breathless and paralyzed. They create deformation in our roots and cut off the life source of our being.

How do you bounce back when the weight of settling for who and what is said from others has overtaken you? Settling comes from a myriad of decisions that we refuse to confront. Confess your sin to one another and watch God breathe life back into the dry ground and restore the fullness of who you were before the foundation of the world. Who are you? You should ask that question.

My vulnerabilities and weaknesses got the best me. I confess, I settled in the weight. I settled so much that the heaviness of mistaken identity, a seed trying to be dislodged by storms, and the pain of a root trying to be dug up created warfare. The weight and settling in it had come for my purpose and my destiny. It attacked every area of my life, until I gave it to The One who had already defeated it. The weight of the settle of life weighed me down where I thought there was not return, BUT GOD.

"Wherefore seeing we also are compassed about with so great a cloud of witnesses, let us lay aside every weight, and the sin which doth so easily beset us, and let us run with patience the race that is set before us." - HEBREWS 12:1

He cuts off every branch in me that bears no fruit, while every branch that does bear fruit he prunes so that it will be even more fruitful. - JOHN 15:2

A seed will never mistake its identity. For when the root of the seed speaks it will bear and be everything that it was intended to become. When a seed is planted it knows what it shall become and the transitions that will take place to manifest its true purpose. Regardless of the type of dirt, location or its environment the external elements will never be able to compromise what is on the inside of the seed. This seed is not worried about imitating another seed. Once the seed begin to grow, its true identity will be revealed. Therefore, as seeds of Christ, His characteristics and His life story tell us what we will encounter as believer. The seed knows how to prepare for the storm; because The Master Gardener has already shown us the plan.

Seeds are prepared for storms. My seed interceded for me. I had just found out about my divorce. The words were piercing. I remember my voice saying, "I can't feel me breathe. I can't breathe." My chest was tight. My tears were uncontrollable. I thought I would pass out right there. I drove home and sat in the carport for about an hour before I could muster up strength to walk into the house. My mom met me at the door and I walked past her. Making it to my room, I crawled onto the bed like a wounded cat circling and sobbing, searching for a soft spot to lie down comfortably.

> **JOHN 15:2**
>
> He cuts off every branch in me that bears no fruit, while every branch that does bear fruit he prunes so that it will be even more fruitful.

Days and weeks went by and no sleep. I went to the doctor because my illness was active again. My body was failing again. I began to abuse alcohol and medications daily to numb the feelings of rejection, pain, suicide, loneliness and embarrassment. Every day after work I would visit a girlfriend's house to drink then pass out on her floor. She never judged me; for she too had come through a similar situation. God will put you around those of like minds to support you while you are going through the storm. She would always tell me "this is not the way to handle this." She would never drink with me; instead she would walk away to her room and pray in silence. God will place people in your life that will become a sounding board for you in the time of trouble.

God always has a plan when we think we are throwing in the towel. I sat at the kitchen counter one evening, alone, starting my second bottle. There were nights I didn't think I would wake up. Perhaps I did not want to. Yet, there were times, drunker than drunk, that I could hear my seed (my spirit) praying in tongues. He was interceding for me when I couldn't muster up a prayer. Romans 8: 26 does say, "In the same way, the Spirit helps us in our weakness. We do not know what we ought to pray for, but the Spirit himself intercedes for us through wordless groans."

One day, I went to the liquor store and walked out with four boxes full of all types of alcohol. The store was going out of business, so I thought this was a great opportunity for me to load up. I promised God I would never purchase another bottle of course when I drank the last one. How many times have me made a promise that this would be the last day, last relationship, last drink, and last drug? Day in and out I found myself passed out in that same spot.

I took my medication, crushed a few pills and shook them it into my glass of wine. I whispered to God, "Are you done with me?" As I sobbed, tears running done my face, rehearsing dramas past, I heard the word, "Enough." I looked up because I recognized that voice. I pushed the glass in front of me away and sat up. I heard His voice again, like a stern father, who was sick and tired of my crying and fits. "Enough," HE said again. I stood up this time sober in mind and spirit.

For we do not have a high priest who is unable to empathize with our weaknesses, but we have one who has been tempted in every way, just as we are--yet he did not sin. - HEB. 4:15

Despite life's situations, The Original Seed (Holy Spirit) holds me to my true identity in Christ. No matter who has walked away and what the diagnoses is, it can't negate why I was created. It is these rare moments that the storms of life push the root of the seed to take over the territory of the enemy. God allowed the struggles of life to strengthen the root of who I am.

If you allow life to dictate who you are, you will forget that you have a purpose and a destiny. As a seed of Christ is our responsibility to not forget who we are and whose we are. We are a precious commodity, a rare jewel that was purchased with the blood of Jesus Christ. First Peter 2:9 is as true for you as it is for me, "But you are a chosen people, a royal priesthood, a holy nation, God's special possession, that you may declare the praises of him who called you out of darkness into his wonderful light."

I started telling you about the Spotted Touch-Me-Not flower earlier. The flower is from the balsam plant family whose ripe seed capsules open explosively when touched, scattering seeds over some distance. The Touch-Me-Not is called a jewel weed because it is born with a projectile seed; and it grows in shaded and dark areas like underneath bridges, where it's hard to detect sunshine. Without light the flower will not exceed four feet in height. However, if it peaks through and catches the glimpse of sunlight it will grow over six feet tall.

The strongest seeds are those that can go through the storm and survive. Your survival is based on the depth of your root. Yes, you experienced the storm, but the storm made your roots grow deeper. The storm reveals that the weapons of your warfare which are still mighty through the pulling down of strongholds. It was in the struggles of divorce, addiction, rejection, family problems that God revealed my true identity.

Second Corinthians 10:4-5 reminds us that we have to be vigilant in coming against those things that threaten that identity. " (For the weapons of our warfare are not carnal, but mighty through God to the pulling down of strong holds ;) Casting down imaginations, and every high thing that exalted itself against the knowledge of God, and bringing into captivity every thought to the obedience of Christ."

There is a Spanish proverb that says, "They had buried us, but they didn't know we were seeds." Trust my experience to know that God is not yet done with you. Even through disease, divorce, addiction God will speak through your storm and demand you to come out. He has not left you and in this moment, He is restoring your faith and who you were before life - happened. God refuses to allow any situation to overwhelm or overcome you and who you are to be. There is purpose rising in you!

Allow me to whisper into your spirit - ENOUGH! No more drowning yourself in the tears of sorrows, past situations, old relationships. Walk away and BE OKAY. They have taken you as far as they could. Now is the time to allow God to guide you the rest of the way. Shoot forth your seed - the seed of the Holy Spirit. Claiming every city and state.

I am now the Youth and Young adult pastor as well and Life and Health Coach for college students at the University of Oregon. Just like the young man I met in a correctional facility years ago, God uses me regularly to speak life, His Word and His Power into young lives. I am planted to impact a new generation of seed; and prayerfully a generation that will become warriors for Christ. I am also the Founder of "Launch So You Can Live" – School of Leadership for Women. Teaching women how to define and develop their self-worth through Christian principles. I also co-direct various youth mentor programs for middle schools and high school students. What were you planted for? What have the years of hard tilling and plowing, and drought prepared you to do? The labor is yet plenteous.

Life will bring its tests and trials, where dirt will be tossed, but we have a gardener who is God The Father who is watching over us day and night. No weapon formed against us shall be able to prosper and every tongue that is spoken over us contrary to God's plan is condemned. No matter what comes your way in this season declare:

- I will take root and allow the Holy Spirit to take me deeper.
- I will take over the territory that God has given to me.
- I will shoot forth the seeds that are that are planted and purposed in my spirit.

KIMBERLY'S PRAYER

Dear Heavenly Father;

We thank you that You have purposed us for this season. That Your Holy Spirit saturates the ground that we walk on. Your Spirit fills the cracks of pain and uncertainty. You are bringing forth the seed that you have promised. God, I thank you for trusting us enough to create the storms to come, the land to be tossed, the roots to be troubled so that You could maximize Your growth in us.

God, even the tears ran like a raging river at times, we thank you for choosing us for such a difficult assignment. Your promise of blessings and growth is upon us in this season. We are destined to be part of Your next move in the earth. And so, God, we ask that You help us not to be distracted by the external factors of life or relationships. We ask that You help us discern the weeds that are choking our divinity, purpose, destiny, assignment and calling. We ask that You increase our spiritual vision so that we remain focused on You. .

God, I pray that we remember to always go into our secret and quiet place to capture the revelation that only comes from You. God let us be bold enough and prepared enough to bear the fruit of the Spirit, to blossom where You plant us, to take root in Your Kingdom and to destroy every stronghold that comes against us and therefore comes against You.

God in this place, in this realm we will shoot forth the seeds of Jesus' blood; His hope, peace, and love. We pray the fire of God, deliverance and salvation will overwhelm the land.

In Jesus name we pray.

Amen!

God's Call For Me To Manifest Now

JOURNALING INVITATION – E CLAUDETTE FREEMAN

For the poor shall never cease out of the land: therefore, I command thee, saying, Thou shalt open thine hand wide unto thy brother, to thy poor, and to thy needy, in thy land.

DEUTERONOMY 15:11

Open thy mouth for the dumb in the cause of all such as are appointed to destruction. Open thy mouth, judge righteously, and plead the cause of the poor and needy.

PROVERBS 31: 8-9

As I face this page, I bravely admit that I have hidden behind the pretty dress of safe and comfortable ministry. Behind that dress, I have run from God's assignment for my life. I commit to that assignment by writing it here:

_____

_____

_____

_____

_____

_____

_____

_____

_____

_____

_____

_____

_____

_____

_____

_____

_____

_____

_____

_____

_____

_____

_____

I open my hand. I open my mouth. I open my spirit. For those in need shall never cease. My seasons thus far have prepared me for:

_____

_____

_____

_____

_____

_____

_____

_____

_____

_____

_____

_____

_____

_____

_____

_____

_____

_____

_____

_____

_____

_____

_____

As I meditate on the power of a woman in radical, revolutionary ministry within the church which is herself; I meditate on a vision of God before me. In this vision, I bow before Him. He extends His right hand to me and gives me an envelope. As, I rise I open and read these words of promise about my purpose:

_____

_____

_____

_____

_____

_____

_____

_____

_____

_____

_____

_____

_____

_____

_____

_____

_____

_____

_____

_____

_____

_____

_____

_____

_____

Afterword and Prayer

You Win In Purpose
Tania Maxwell-Carroll

As a little girl growing up in a family of twelve, and being one of the younger children, I learned early on that this goes with that. Surely, if that experience caused that; then this experience would cause this. You also learn to find your way in one community full of various personalities, thoughts, visions, desires and emotions. You find yourself looking for your place; a spot where you could fit in yet be unique. You often looked for ways to be the one noticed.

Life has a way of teaching you that there are consequences with being the one. Whether it is being the smart one, the dumb one, the pretty one or even the ugly one. Even if it is being the scary one. I was, at some point or another, a little bit of them all. I was afraid of everything and everyone. My big sisters fought for me. Heck, my little sister fought for me. I was afraid. My parents didn't help my fears. My mother had a loud, strong voice and she wasn't afraid to use it. My dad had a gentle stern voice and a stern hand. He used both to discipline his dozen, even if there were times (as the old saying goes) he would have to beat the "snot" out of us before we learned.

The other one we are often called to be is the chosen one. Chosen to do something small or big for God. Chosen to speak a word in or out of season. Chosen to touch the untouchable. The chosen one often is doubted, questioned and ridiculed. The chosen one runs. Yet there is a community of believers, chosen ones, who have moved into their calling after having The Father, in His own way discipline us into alignment. The chosen recognize the chosen. Often, God must persuade us into alignment through difficult circumstances. Those circumstances may come later in life, some present themselves in our youth.

Seeing the strength of my sisters, I learned to get over a lot of my fears and stand up for myself. Until, a circumstance. I was waiting for the school bus, when out of nowhere I was run over by a van. I was once more afraid of life. The accident left me with a broken pelvis, and a Foley catheter attached to my leg to use the bathroom. The doctors were not sure I would be able to have children. They also were not confident that I would walk without a limp.

Fear can be crippling. Fear does not stop the will of God. I am the mother of two. My career was spent moving from one emergency to another, moving equipment and bodies, not hindered by a limp. Your fear cannot and should not stop your season of walking into your assignment, despite the circumstances that come to dictate otherwise.

Ecclesiastes 3:1 says for everything there is a season. My season of fear came to an end. I learned that I could not pursue purpose without being shaken by life's trials and tribulations. Romans 8:28 tells us that all things work together for the good of them who are the called, according to His purpose. God has a plan for me. God has a plan for you.

It doesn't matter how you got here: out of wedlock, adoption or even rape; God has a plan for your life. He knew you before you were in your mother's womb. Jeremiah 29:11 reminds us that God knows the thoughts that He has towards us, thoughts of peace and not evil - an expected end.

You weren't meant to go through life aimlessly, trying to figure out who you are and what you're supposed to be doing. The enemy doesn't want you to operate in your purpose. He doesn't want you to win; so, when you were a little girl he set up distractions and traps to deter you from your destiny. I know that you can't forget the molestation, the rape or the bullying, the beatings and name calling from your childhood that you carried into your adult life. You struggled with the rejection. You gave into the drugs, pride, lust, depression, alcohol, curses and wrong choices. You fed into the negativity so long that you believed the devil's lies.

There is truth, however, that you must affirm over your life. God created you for a purpose. A purpose to resemble Him in the Earth. To love unconditionally. To speak up for those with no voice. To serve the lost, the least, and the left out. To minister to another's pain from your own. No matter what IT was – it has not won. I want to declare to you today, that You win. Your past is behind you. You are not the what the devil – or anyone else - says you are. You are a winner, and everything attached to you wins. You are the head and not the tail.

Genesis 1:26 tells us that we were created in the image of God. You were fearfully and wonderfully made according to Psalm 139. You are not confined or defined by man's opinion of you. You are a designer's original from God, and no one else can wear what The Father has fashioned for you!

Live on purpose! You were born for and with a purpose. God uses it all. He used an old woman named Sarah to birth Isaac as a sign of His promise. He used a harlot named Rahab to bring forth the lineage of Jesus. He used a virgin girl named Mary to bring the Savior into the world. He used an orphan girl named Esther to save her people. God has purpose for you too.

It's your season to be actively victorious in purpose!

NOW FATHER,

I come to You as humbly and sincerely as I know how. Lord, I give you honor and praise. I first ask for forgiveness of sins; they are ever before me. Create in me a clean heart, renew a right spirit in me. I ask that You bind up the hand of the enemy, allow no weapon that's formed against me and Your daughters to prosper. I ask You Lord to have mercy on me.

God as Your daughters, give us teachable spirits, open our hearts and minds that we will receive You and Your word.

God, I ask that You use us for Your Glory. Father God allow those that read this book to see You. Let them see Your hand behind every word. Let them see You as The Author and Finisher of their lives. Let them be renewed in the worship.

Father, I pray that they will be refreshed by the words and begin new life realigned to and for Your purpose. Father, I ask that You heal every wounded woman, whether the hurt was spiritual, physical, mental or emotional. I plead the blood of Jesus over every broken heart, every broken promise, every broken spirit and every broken mind and will. Every assignment of the enemy is cancelled in the name of Jesus.

Lord God, I ask that You move mightily in the souls, spirits and hearts of Your women, that they will seek You daily for their called assignments and walk in their God-given destiny. That they will no longer sit on the sidelines of ministry.

That they will begin to speak life into every dry bone in their personal valley. That they will no longer see themselves as just a pretty face. That they will no longer see themselves as just a wife, daughter, mother, sister or friend. That they will no longer see themselves as rejected and unworthy. That they will no longer see themselves as just their former selves. That they will no longer see themselves under the definition of a negative word.

But God, allow Your daughters to see themselves as whole, powerful and anointed beings. To see themselves as daughters of the Most High God, who were created to soar as eagles. To see themselves as gifts in Your Kingdom. Father let them know that the price that You paid for them was worth all that they are and still will become.

I Intercede on behalf of Your women. Those that don't even know or remember their name. I intercede on behalf of those that have forgotten who they were, who they were called to be. I intercede on their behalf. I command this book to bless them and cause them to know You and the call on their lives.

Father, I ask that if there is anything that is not like You, that is not pleasing to You in the lives of these contributing authors, the publishing company team and those who are reading these words right now - remove it. God even if they love it. Even if they think they can't live without it. God cause them to know that it is You, and You, alone that they can't live without. It is You that loves them unconditionally. It is You that gives them life. God it is You.

God, I ask that you bless every gift that's been placed in this book. The vision and the visionary behind it. Give them clarity of focus in every area of their lives. God let doors be opened, and opportunities be realized. Lord touch each family and ministry that penned these words and those that will encounter these words that they will be blessed ever the more. Every prophetic word will be made manifest and there will be no backlash and no hinderances. God, we give You ALL THE GLORY!

Thank you, Lord, for being our God and allowing us to be Your people. Thank you, Father, for being Jehovah Jireh, providing for us. Thank you for being Jehovah Shalom, giving us peace. Thank you for being Jehovah Rapha, our healer. Thank You God for being our God in every situation and in all things.

In Jesus Name.

Amen.

The Women Serving Beyond the Pretty Dress

ANIKA WILSON BROWN
www.anikawilsonbrown.com

Anika Wilson Brown is an amazing woman of God, fireball transformation specialist, no holds barred speaker to the project. Imparting ancient spiritual truths with contemporary flair, Anika is an expert on manifesting dreams into reality. She inspires audiences by uniquely integrating proven therapeutic techniques and spiritual principles to breakthrough past pain and activate Divine potential. One of the most sought-after speakers on the topic of merging faith and psychotherapy, Anika has spoken on diverse platforms, ranging from arena-sized gatherings to one-on-one small sessions.

TANIA MAXWELL CARROLL
www.facebook.com/tania.maxwellcarroll

Minister Tania Maxwell Carroll is the First Lady of Greater Antioch Missionary Baptist Church, her service in that capacity and as Church Administrator epitomizes touching those in need. She does so regularly through workshops and sermonic messages across the country, hosting Brown Bag Bible Studies, and through the non-profit she founded and leads, The Community C.A.R.E. Center, a healthcare resource and referral center, that utilizes funds for preventative maintenance of hypertension, diabetes as well as screening and counseling for HIV/AIDS.

E. CHANTAYE WATSON
www.facebook.com/apeaceofvictory

Anointed to be a mouthpiece and scribe for God - Minister, Poet, Author, Motivator and Artist, E. Chantaye Watson has done so with abandon in her writings and on various platforms before men, women and children. But most importantly, she has yielded herself to the complete will of God in her life. This yielding has taken her on a journey that has not been easy, yet, has been instrumental in who she is today and where God is taking her. She has exercised her creative talent as the Creative Director for 4 Christian magazines. She additionally ministers through another assignment given to her by God to encourage through the art of journaling to bring healing to workshop participants while glorifying God in their stories, testimonies, songs, prayers and other writings.

CRYSTAL LEE
cdlee1257@gmail.com

Crystal Lee is a retired License Practical Nurse, her career spanned over 41 years. She has spent the last 28 years working in the HIV/AIDS arena. She is a Community Advocate and Health Educator. For those who will engage BEYOND THE PRETTY DRESS, Crystal shares how critical the presence of the church is in battling the health, family, community and spiritual effects of HIV and AIDS.

TRICKA BROWN
www.facebook.com/wordoffaithcm

Tricka D. Brown serves as the Pastor of Word of Faith Christian Ministries and the Executive Director of Word of Faith Community Development Corporation. With over 25 years of experience in the mortgage industry, this has given her a chance to give back to her community by helping others purchase their first home. In BEYOND THE PRETTY DRESS, Pastor Brown shares her story of overcoming depression and allowing God to convert her inside before changing her outside appearance. She shares the story of her great fall, which also was the push to give her life to God.

CAROL WILLIAMS
http://www.icaresolutions.website/

Elder Carol J. Williams is the founder of I CARE SOLUTIONS, LLC., an organization formed to improve the lives of the broken, outcast and disenfranchised of society. Elder Carol is an author, ministry leader, and (former) radio talk show host. In our upcoming release, BEYOND THE PRETTY DRESS, she shares her story of overcoming the throngs of grief and suicide to trusting the will of God.

DEBRA WADLINGTON HOUSE
https://m.facebook.com/debrajhouse

Pastor Debra Wadlington House, CEO and Founder of A Sister's Touch Ministries and Ask Pastor Deb Recovery Café, provides leadership, vision, mobilization, and training to families, specializing in Women's Ministries and Recovery. Pastor Debra House has a "Passion for Victory."

MARIA PINKSTON BAZILE
http://www.thesoulsanctuary.org

Maria holds an undergraduate degree in Journalism from Howard University in Washington, D.C., a Master's degree in Guidance and Counseling from Saint Thomas University in Miami, Florida, and a Ph.D. in Family Therapy from Nova Southeastern University in Davie, Florida. While in college she interned in New York City with famed African American publicist Terrie Williams, she went on to land her first job as a public relations assistant for boxing promoter Don King in Oakland Park, Florida. After leaving the PR field she went on to pursue a career in education and counseling. She is currently employed in Atlanta, Georgia where serves a Behavior Specialist. She is the Founder and CEO of The Soul Sanctuary, Inc. a not for profit 501(c)3 dedicated to promoting healthy relationships and violence -free families by the teaching and training of the faith community.

CYTERIA FREEMAN
www.facebook.com/cyteriaf

Rev. Cyteria Freeman is a reverend, mother, grandmother and lover of Christ flowing completely in the five-fold ministry. After years of struggling in the under-belly of addiction, she has become a minister of the gospel and co-host of a radio show. She went from being a school drop-out to a college student excelling in studies and earning a Bachelor's degree. She is Founder and President of Unlimited Miracles Ministry and Co-Founder of Victoriously Overcoming Substance Abuse Radio Ministry.

KATHEI MCCOY
http://coachkathei.com

Kathei McCoy is an ordained minister, Certified Life Coach, Author and Speaker. McCoy has a passionate mission to write stories, speak messages and teach principles that empower women and girls to live in the fierceness of truth and freedom. She is the author of the book, "To Mothers Raising Sons; How to Love them to Life Instead of Death."

CHOSEN THUMMIMS
https://www.facebook.com/chosen.thummims

Min. Chosen U. Thummims, is a mother of three, and grandmother to one grandson. The youngest of four children, she is a native of the sunny Miami, FL. In 2000, ministry lead her to South Carolina where she has been ministering for 22 years to the homeless, teen intervention, as well as motivational speaking geared toward women's empowerment and healing.

YVETTE FREEMAN ROWLAND
www.facebook.com/yvette.f.rowland

Yvette Rowland is a post-secondary instructor. Her disciplines are psychology, business, criminal justice and adult education. Helping others to achieve their aspirational goals of higher education has been her passion for more than a decade. Additionally, Yvette is a Department of Treasury employee. In our upcoming release, BEYOND THE PRETTY DRESS, she shares her journey to love and accept her "imperfect" "peculiar" self ... saying; there IS indeed room at the cross for even me.

JANICE LEWIS
http://projecthopeglobal.org

Missionary Janice Lewis is a highly energetic Missionary with a Master's in Theology who understands the Power of God to change lives. Ms. Lewis' has a joyous Spirit and uses prayer, relationships and networking to fulfill church objectives and to meet outreach needs. She willingly assumes physical and spiritual tasks and responsibilities and actively seeks out ways in which to contribute. Her background encompasses positions at multi-billion-dollar foundation and two national newspapers. Solid writing skills and well-deserved reputation for proposing new ideas and driving projects to completion. Brings passionate commitment to excellence, sense of urgency and upbeat, positive personality into any religious organization.

KIMBERLY MCGREW
www.kimmcgrewspeaks.com

Kimberly McGrew, Pastor, teacher, trainer, life/health coach, writer and motivational speaker, shares profound truths born out of her personal experiences in a manner that inspires everyone that encounter her. She is the co-author of "Finishing Strong," a workbook and journal on personal goal setting; while maintaining the audacity to speak peace during the storm. She empowers communities through wellness techniques as CEO of Kimistry Wellness and Prevention as a Holistic Health Practitioner.

www.ingramcontent.com/pod-product-compliance
Lightning Source LLC
Chambersburg PA
CBHW052052090426
42739CB00010B/2140